Fast Desserts

Fast Desserts

by

Mary Berry

PIATKUS

My thanks to Clare Blunt for her help in developing and testing the recipes in this book; and to her children, Timothy and Kate, for tasting them.

© 1983 Mary Berry
First published in 1983 by
Judy Piatkus (Publishers) Limited of Loughton, Essex

British Library Cataloguing in Publication Data

Berry, Mary, 1935–
   Fast desserts
   1. Desserts
   I. Title
   641.8′6   TX773

   ISBN 0-86188-404-3

Typeset by Phoenix Photosetting, Chatham
Printed and bound by Garden City Press, Letchworth, Herts.

Contents

Illustrations

INTRODUCTION

Who wants pudding? Almost everybody, as far as I know. Certainly my family wouldn't be without something to round off the meal. Puddings improve the quality of life. Most people love them, especially children and those of us who are still children at heart. Look at the good things that go into them. Fruit, cream, sugar, eggs. There are puddings that are light and refreshing after a substantial main course, or hot and satisfying to follow a salad meal; some of them ooze cream and richness for the frankly greedy, others subtly blend flavours for the sophisticated palate. No meal is complete without pudding.

Who has time to make puddings nowadays? The simple answer is, anybody who cares. Modern cooking methods, improved ingredients, new ideas in equipment, have opened up fresh horizons in the kitchen both for the housewife who combines a career with entertaining at home, or for the busy mother cooking for a hungry family. Preparation of food has never been quicker and easier than it is today, ingredients have never been so varied, and the wise cook makes the most of her advantages.

Few of us today can devote as much time as we would like to cooking, so the emphasis is on speed. None of the recipes here takes more than 15 minutes to prepare or over 1 hour to cook, and some are a good deal faster than that. All these puddings have been tried and tested over the years. Some have been handed down in my family, others are regularly demanded by my own children. In all of them the object is ease and speed of preparation.

Let me say right from the beginning that fast does *not* mean instant. Fast means being well organised, having a good store cupboard stocked with pudding ingredients, making preparations in advance if possible, thinking ahead. It does not mean going out and buying a supply of 'instant' food.

It does mean taking advantage of new developments that are making fast food faster all the time. New soft fats have cut down the time and labour of mixing, processors and blenders have eliminated the tedious and time-consuming chores of food preparation.

7

Think ahead

Thinking ahead is all important and a little time spent on planning can save hours of work, and a lot of money. If you are cooking for a family, plan meals every few days to avoid waste. Make more than you need for one meal and you will have some left to freeze for another day.

Make more than enough rice pudding for the family meal and you will have some left for a pear condé or Connaught rice tomorrow. Simple stewed apricots can be made into a fool later with the addition of cream. Make mousse to fill one large dish, plus several small individual ones to go into the freezer. Keep back some of the fruit salad to make trifle. Any creamy gâteau that remains can reappear from the fridge – but do cut it into slices and serve it on individual plates so that it does not look like leftovers!

The cook in a hurry soon thinks out her own ways of saving time. My recipes, even the traditional ones, have been adapted to easier and quicker methods. Where possible I like to prepare everything in one bowl, and this is where the new soft fats are invaluable. If a recipe calls for melted fat, then mix in the other ingredients in the same pan.

Electric mixers, food processors, blenders or liquidisers have revolutionised the kitchen. They have done away with hours of preparation – chopping, whisking, creaming, mixing, puréeing – and opened up a whole new world to the fast cook. The processor is the newest, probably the most expensive, but definitely the most versatile. It is in fact so fast that you must stand over it and not let it do too much! Use it with care for puddings and cakes; an all-in-one sponge, for instance, should be just blended. When chopping nuts use the processor just long enough to retain the texture, not to make a powder.

If you are making a mousse or a soufflé with the electric mixer, first stand the bowl and whisk in very hot water for a few moments and there is no need to whisk the mixture over hot water as we used to do.

Make your electric equipment work for you. Keep the processor or blender standing ready for use always, not stored away in a cupboard when you will think twice about using it. Even washing up, high on most cooks' list of least favourite, most time-wasting jobs, need present no problems if you exercise a little ingenuity. Before you use the processor, think out the recipe and do things in the logical order. You can perhaps start the pudding by coarsely grating the chocolate for decoration, then tip it out and put the remainder of the ingredients in the bowl. Or first whip cream, put it in the piping bag and use the bowl for the pudding mixture *without* washing it up first. If you get into the habit of thinking like this you will be surprised by the amount of time you save.

Quick money-saving ideas

There are a lot of money-saving dodges that are well worth knowing.

Dried milk, for instance, is cheaper than fresh, and it keeps well too.

If a recipe calls for cream you can nearly always use about half cream and half yogurt. Home made yogurt is far cheaper than bought. You can make your own in a machine or in a wide-necked vacuum flask. Here is my recipe:

1 pint (600 ml) milk
1 tablespoon bought yogurt
1 heaped tablespoon dried milk powder

Heat the milk to boiling, then cool in a bowl of cold water to about 112°F, 44°C (hot bath temperature). Put the yogurt in a bowl with the milk and whisk in the dried milk powder. Cover and put either in a linen cupboard overnight or in a vacuum flask for 6 hours. Of course, if you have one, use a yogurt-making kit instead.

Make your own cream too. I make it in the blender in about 30 seconds from fresh unsalted butter. It works out at about half the price of cream from the shops. It can be used in all recipes that call for single cream. This is how I do it:

½ lb (225 g) unsalted butter
½ pint (300 ml) milk
scant level teaspoon powdered gelatine

Cut the butter into small pieces. Put the milk in a pan and sprinkle on the gelatine and leave for 3 minutes. Add the butter and heat until the butter has just melted. Pour into the blender and switch on to maximum for 30 seconds until blended. Pour into a jug and chill, stirring from time to time. These quantities make just under 1 pint (568 ml) cream. Or, instead of cream, try serving luxury custard. This is a half and half mixture of cream and pouring custard (the bought kind).

Use fresh fruit in season when it is at its cheapest. You can often find damaged fruit in your local market that is perfectly suitable for puddings or fruit salads when you do not need to produce perfect whole fruit. A melon, for example. may be discoloured on one side, but cut away the blemished part and the rest will go into a fruit salad or garnish a dish. Our village shop often has a box outside offering cheap lemons or fully ripe fruit.

Take advantage of what you can get. Having planned your cooking you can still be flexible and save yourself money at the same time.

I don't nowadays make sugar syrup for fruit salad. I simply layer the fruits in caster sugar. And when you are making fruit salad, do the citrus fruits first, then toss in the rest. The citrus fruits used like this should stop the others discolouring.

If you are making a pudding with a pronounced flavour, you can always use margarine. I now use butter only when I want a definite buttery taste.

Don't throw away stale bread, cake or biscuits. Make breadcrumbs and store them in the freezer to use for, say, apple charlotte or St Andrews layer. Broken biscuits can be used for chocolate heaven or chocolate tiffin and crumbled digestives make digestive crust for cheesecakes and other puddings. Soft biscuits can be freshened up in the oven. Keep pieces of stale cake to put in trifles.

When you use the juice of a lemon or orange make sure you use the rind as well. It keeps well in caster sugar in the larder and can be used for flavouring and decoration.

Don't despise squashy bananas, but use them in a hot banana pudding. Or fry them. *Don't* use them in fruit salad.

What's in store

Fast cookery relies very much on ingredients that can be quickly assembled, and that are readily available when you need them. There is nothing particularly fast about a recipe that cooks in half an hour if you have to rush out to the shops at the last minute to buy something essential. Worse still if an ingredient you need is missing and the shops are closed and your dinner party guests are on the doorstep.

So, once again, do plan in advance. And do keep good supplies on hand. It follows that planning starts in the freezer and the larder. If they are well stocked, you can greet emergencies like unexpected visitors, or a sudden influx of the children's friends, with serene confidence.

The *freezer* is invaluable for stocking all manner of pudding ingredients, as well as finished puddings themselves. When you are making a pudding that freezes well it pays to make two, use one at once and freeze the other for use later. My attitude to the freezer has changed over the years. I used to stock it indiscriminately with finished dishes and no definite plans for using them. Nowadays, particularly in the case of ready made dishes like American apple cake which need only thawing and perhaps the addition of cream, I like to plan in advance and to know on what particular occasion I am going to serve a certain dish. Basics like ice cream are a different matter. You can always find a use for them.

The freezer makes it possible to have a stock of your favourite fruits available all the year round. Buy when they are in season and at their best and cheapest. Try the local markets for bargains, or take advantage of the pick-your-own offers made by growers in your neighbourhood. Picking can be a good day out for the whole family and you get first class fruit at very competitive prices.

Best of all the summer fruits for freezing are raspberries, with loganberries and blackcurrants coming a close second. Wild strawberries freeze well too. Yes, *wild* strawberries. I have a few in the garden and I freeze the fruit to use for decorating puddings. You *can* freeze ordinary strawberries, but to my mind it is not worth the trouble. They all too easily turn to a mush when thawed. Best use I know for frozen strawberries is to fill a bought flan case with jelly and drop in partly thawed strawberries when the jelly is lukewarm. This goes down very well with children.

Gooseberries freeze well whole for pies and crumbles, but for fools and ices it is best to cook and sieve them and freeze the purée, so that they take up less room in the freezer. You can do the same with the last pickings of the raspberries. Use the purée to make fool or sorbet, or serve with added icing sugar as a sauce with ice cream.

Apples are perhaps the most useful fruit of all, and they don't cost much. In a good apple year the owners of trees are often only too glad to give away surplus apples, and windfalls are usually free anyway. I certainly freeze all the windfalls from our own trees.

Apples are best cooked before freezing. Peel them straight into a bucket of salt water (one handful of salt to a bucket of water). Rinse them in cold water and cook to a pulp in a preserving pan with just a little water. Sweeten them at the end of the cooking with 2 to 3 oz (50 to 75 g) sugar to 1 lb (450 g) apples. I don't use a lot of sugar because I find my family always add sugar to apple pie anyway.

With some of the purée I make apple pies or crumbles and freeze them in oven glass dishes. Some can be put in ice cream containers (don't fill to the top) and frozen till solid. Next day dip the containers in hot water and the purée will slip out like a jelly. This you can store in the freezer in polythene bags ready for use when you want a pudding in a hurry.

A stock of cream frozen in granules or pieces is very handy to have. It is cheaper than fresh cream and just as good in recipes. Remember the night before to thaw out what you will need. Another cream, one that you can keep in the fridge, comes in aerosol canisters and can be piped directly on to a pudding. It goes a long way but once piped it loses its volume quickly. Children love it.

It goes without saying that a good supply of bought vanilla ice cream more than pays for its space in the freezer. Served with home-made sauces – chocolate, butterscotch, fruit – it makes one of the quickest puddings you can have.

Nuts stored in the freezer will keep perfectly for years, whereas they soon turn rancid on the larder shelf. Store them, either whole or ground, in small polythene bags. Label these and keep them in one large bag. Then when you need a small amount of ground almonds, say, or a few hazelnuts or walnuts for decoration, they are ready to hand to save you a special expedition to the shops.

Store breadcrumbs or biscuit crumbs in polythene bags. Blocks of plain cooking chocolate keep better in the freezer than in the larder.

A well stocked *larder* is the cook's inspiration and joy. Its shelves hold the basics, and the trimmings, for an infinite variety of puddings. Some are very simple. For example, my family love rice pudding and I keep canned rice pudding which needs no more addition than a little butter on top to make a skin.

My children would be content to live indefinitely on canned sliced peaches, so I keep a good supply of those. Large cans are best value. If there is too much for your immediate needs, decant the fruit, use some and freeze the rest. For very special occasions there are canned white peaches, lychees and green figs. In fact any canned fruit with the addition of cream or ice cream makes about as fast a pudding as you could want, and it gives a lift to fresh fruit salad too.

Bought pie fillings – cherry is our favourite – are useful and quick to use. Bought ice cream toppings, as opposed to the home-made ones in the freezer, are expensive but they are very popular with children and a little goes a surprisingly long way. Instant whips have their uses.

Jars of mincemeat are worth keeping. The bought variety is good value if you serve it mixed with apple. Apricot jam is useful for adding to puddings.

I like to keep bought meringue cases and flan cases to bring quickly into service with cream or ice cream and fruit. Sponge fingers dress up a quick pudding. Marshmallows can be put on top of fruit and browned quickly under the grill, or they can be snipped into ice cream and served with fruit. Packet jellies don't take long to set if you top up with ice cubes. Chestnut purée for Monte Bianco or Mont Blanc has its place in the larder.

And I would never be without custard powder. It goes with so many different puddings and it is much less expensive than cream. It is easy to use, and if it turns lumpy a few moments in the processor will put that right.

Make it look good

The presentation of a dish is vitally important. However fresh the ingredients, however well cooked, however mouth-watering the recipe, the result will not be perfect unless you make it look good. A little time taken over the appearance of a dish when it is brought to table is a compliment to your guests and shows you have taken the trouble to please them.

Besides it is fun to present any dish well, and puddings lend themselves to decoration. It need not be elaborate, often simple effects are best. If your pudding contains a particular fruit, then decorate it with the same fruit, using the best specimens you can find. If you are using strawberries or raspberries pick out a few of the best before you start. Fresh leaves of the same fruit can be a most attractive decoration.

Whipped cream finishes off a mousse and if you don't want to pipe it, then just put it on in blobs, one to each serving, perhaps.

Use fresh lemon or orange slices, or grapes brushed with egg white and dipped in caster sugar. Sometimes a dusting of icing sugar is all you need, or a sprinkling of demerara sugar, or grated chocolate. Or use nuts, chopped or whole, desiccated coconut, glacé cherries or angelica. You can even buy 'golden' almonds from Harrods but these are for *very* special occasions. They have silver and coloured ones too.

There is endless scope for imagination and inventiveness in dressing up puddings and it can all be done in a few minutes.

And do please serve hot puddings very hot and cold ones very cold.

Build up a stock of china and glass. Think out what you need with a view to your next birthday or Christmas presents. You may want a new soufflé dish, or a set of ramekins, or all-purpose oven-to-table ware. There is no harm in dropping a few hints to family and friends!

I like all white china and I have acquired a good selection. It is simple and undemanding and its very simplicity enhances the appearance of the pudding itself. Glass dishes too are a favourite with me. To my mind a fruit salad looks its best in a straight sided glass bowl. Oven glass dishes that you use for serving at table *must* be kept bright and shining. This is not difficult. Simply soak the dish as soon as it is empty in hot water and biological washing powder and it will come up sparkling every time.

Finally, the suggestions and ideas here are all part of my own experience over the years and I know that they work. Cooking can be great enjoyment. It is up to you to see that enjoyment is shared by your family and friends and all who come to your table.

OLD-FASHIONED ENGLISH PUDDINGS

In our house we like good old-fashioned hot puddings. Filling they are, of course, but how warm and comforting on a cold day! We eat salad all year round and after such a light main course I make a point of serving a substantial pudding.

These are traditional recipes for puddings known and loved since schooldays and much appreciated by the next generation. They are the recipes our mothers knew, and our mothers took a good deal of time and trouble to prepare them. I have tried to speed them up for today's cooks with easier starts and quicker methods, using modern ingredients.

Perhaps you are making a sponge topping. This was once an elaborate process of creaming butter and sugar with a wooden spoon in a basin. Now you put all the ingredients together into a bowl and mix in minutes in the processor or mixer. Today's soft margarine and cooking fats have revolutionised this branch of cookery. Several small steamed sponge puddings – you can do them in handleless cups – cook much more quickly than one big one. Then for tarts and pies you have your pastry ready to use in the freezer. And I make no apology for including a fast recipe for Christmas pudding – no collection of puddings would be complete without it. This is a genuinely fast recipe, helped by one of today's advantages, shredded suet. We just empty ours out of a packet, our mothers had to chop theirs laboriously with a knife on a wooden board or grate it.

When you want a change from the nourishing delights of treacle tart, apple roly poly or bread and butter pudding, try a hot soufflé. Nothing does more for a cook's reputation than a spectacularly risen golden soufflé straight from the oven. There is no mystery about soufflés. They are quick and cheap and easy to make and the saying is that if you can make a white sauce you can make a soufflé. What you *must* do is have your guests ready to eat it at exactly the moment when it is ready for them. This is never any problem in my family.

15

Bakewell Slice

Really almondy, yet it contains no almonds in the filling. Serve either warm or cold.

Preparation time about 15 minutes
Cooking time about 30 minutes

*6 oz (175 g) pastry crumbs (see page 179), or a small 8-oz (227-g)
    packet shortcrust pastry*
about 1½ tablespoons cold water

Filling
   4 oz (100 g) butter
   4 oz (100 g) caster sugar
   1 egg, beaten
   4 oz (100 g) ground rice
   ½ teaspoon almond essence
   1 heaped tablespoon apricot jam

Heat the oven to 400°F, 200°C, gas mark 6.

Place the pastry crumbs in a bowl and add sufficient water to mix to a firm dough. Roll out thinly on a floured surface and line an 8-inch (20-cm) flan ring, which should be placed on a baking sheet. Prick the base with a fork and leave to rest in the refrigerator for 5 minutes, whilst making the filling.

Heat the butter in a saucepan until it has just melted, but is not brown. Stir in the sugar and cook for a minute, then stir in the egg, ground rice and almond essence.

Spread the jam over the base of the pastry and pour the filling on top. Bake in the oven for about 30 minutes until risen and golden brown. The filling will spring back when lightly pressed with the finger. Take out of the oven and remove the flan ring; leave to cool on a wire rack.

Serves 6

Mincemeat and Apple Tart

Mince pie is always a favourite and I find that adding a large cooking apple keeps it nice and moist. (*Illustrated on the jacket.*)

Preparation time about 10 minutes
Cooking time about 35 to 40 minutes

Pastry
12 oz (350 g) pastry crumbs (see page 179)
about 3 tablespoons cold water

Filling
4 rounded tablespoons mincemeat, or to taste
1 large cooking apple, peeled, cored and sliced

Heat the oven to 400°F, 200°C, gas mark 6.

Place the pastry crumbs in a bowl and add sufficient cold water to mix to a firm dough. Divide the pastry in half and then roll out one piece on a floured surface and use to line an 8-inch (20-cm) enamel plate.

Spread the mincemeat over the pastry and then cover with the layer of apple. Roll out the remaining pastry, cover the tart, and seal the edges firmly. Make two small slits in the centre. Brush the pie with a little water and then sprinkle with granulated sugar.

Bake in the oven for 35 to 40 minutes until the pastry is crisp and golden brown.

Serves 6 to 8

Treacle Tart

I keep breadcrumbs in the freezer, and you can add them frozen to the
syrup – they will soften up if you mash them down against the side of
the pan with a wooden spoon.

Preparation time about 10 minutes
Cooking time about 25 minutes

Pastry
6 oz (175 g) pastry crumbs (see page 179), or a small 8-oz (227-g)
   packet shortcrust pastry
about 1½ tablespoons cold water

Filling
about 9 lightly rounded tablespoons golden syrup
about 9 rounded tablespoons fresh white breadcrumbs
grated rind and juice of half a lemon

Heat the oven to 400°F, 200°C, gas mark 6.

Place the pastry crumbs in a bowl and add sufficient water to mix to a
firm dough. Roll out thinly on a floured surface and line a 9-inch
(22.5-cm) deep flan tin or sandwich tin.

Warm the syrup in a saucepan until runny and stir in the breadcrumbs
and the lemon rind and juice. It is difficult to be accurate when
measuring golden syrup, so if the mixture looks a little thick add more
syrup or if too thin add a few more breadcrumbs.

Pour into the pastry case and bake in the oven for 10 minutes, then
reduce the heat to 375°F, 190°C, gas mark 5 and bake for a further 15
minutes or until the tart is cooked.

Leave to cool in the tin for a little while and then serve warm with lots
of whipped double cream or ice cream.

Serves 8

Blackberry and Apple Sponge

Use fruit in season. Blackberry and apple, gooseberries, blackcurrant or just apple, and for a change, mix with a little mincemeat. Start the fruit cooking in the oven whilst you quickly make the sponge. Very popular on a cold day when the main course is a salad or sparse! Use a shallow dish and it will be cooked in an hour.

Preparation time about 10 minutes
Cooking time about 1 hour

8 oz (225 g) cooking apples, peeled, cored and sliced
8 oz (225 g) blackberries
2 to 3 oz (50 to 75 g) granulated sugar
4 oz (100 g) soft margarine
4 oz (100 g) caster sugar
2 eggs
4 oz (100 g) self-raising flour
1 level teaspoon baking powder

Heat the oven to 350°F, 180°C, gas mark 4. Grease a 2-pint (a good litre) ovenproof dish, and put in the apples and blackberries and sprinkle with the sugar. Put into the oven whilst preparing the sponge.

Put the margarine, sugar, eggs, flour and baking powder in a bowl and beat well for a minute until well blended. Remove the dish from the oven and spread the batter over the fruit. Bake in the centre of the oven for about an hour or until the sponge is golden brown, well risen and will spring back when lightly touched. Serve hot with custard.

Serves 6

Apple Roly Poly

A real winter pudding – rather fattening, but always popular with the family.

Preparation time about 12 to 15 minutes
Cooking time 40 minutes

8 oz (225 g) self-raising flour
pinch of salt
4 oz (100 g) shredded suet
about 8 tablespoons cold water, to mix
2 tablespoons demerara sugar
2 cooking apples, peeled, cored and sliced

Heat the oven to 400°F, 200°C, gas mark 6, and lightly flour a baking tray.

Mix together the flour, salt and suet in a bowl, add sufficient cold water to make a soft but not sticky dough, and then knead lightly. Roll out on a floured working surface to a 10-inch (25-cm) square, and spread the sugar to within 1 inch (2.5 cm) of the edge. Lay on the apple slices and then roll up loosely and press the edges firmly together with the rolling pin.

Lift onto a baking tray and cook for about 40 minutes until golden brown. Transfer to a warm serving dish and serve in slices with a spoonful of golden syrup on each portion.

Serves 6

Royal Lemon Pudding

With a light sponge on top and a sharp sauce underneath, this is one of the best puddings that I know – and it's made from ingredients already in the larder plus 1 lemon. To keep hot, remove from the oven, leave in the meat tin of water, but don't cover, otherwise the sauce will curdle.

Preparation time about 10 minutes
Cooking time about 45 to 50 minutes

2 oz (50 g) soft margarine
6 oz (175 g) caster sugar
2 eggs, separated
grated rind and juice of 1 large lemon
2 oz (50 g) self-raising flour
½ pint (300 ml) milk

Heat the oven to 375°F, 190°C, gas mark 5. Well butter an ovenproof dish of about 1½ to 2 pint (900 ml to 1 litre) capacity.

Beat the margarine, sugar, egg yolks, lemon rind and juice until smooth. Stir in the flour and gradually add the milk. At this stage the mixture looks a bit curdled, but do not worry.

Whisk the egg whites until they form soft peaks, fold into the mixture and pour into the dish. Stand dish in a meat tin and then pour in sufficient hot water to come half way up the sides of the dish.

Bake for about 45 to 50 minutes until a pale golden brown on top, when the pudding will be light and spongy and have its own lemon sauce underneath. Serve at once.

Serves 4

Bread and Butter Pudding

I don't think of this as an economical pudding. In our house it is a great favourite when I know every one is hungry. It is best left to stand, if time allows, but as long as the bread is fresh it seems to work without standing. I use medium sliced bread for speed.

While reading this copy through, this is as far as I got at about twelve – lunch is at one. I had a passion to make this as it was a freezing January day, so I set about gathering the ingredients. No dried fruit, so I lined the dish with buttered bread, put a thick layer of mincemeat on top then a layer of bread and butter uppermost. I then poured over the eggs and milk, and in about 35 minutes I had a glorious pudding!

Preparation time about 15 minutes
Cooking time about 40 minutes

about 3 oz (75 g) butter
9 thin slices white bread, crusts removed
4 oz (100 g) sultanas and currants, mixed
grated rind of 1 lemon
3 oz (75 g) demerara sugar
¾ pint (450 ml) milk
2 eggs

Thoroughly grease a 2½-pint (1.4-litre) ovenproof dish. Melt the butter in a saucepan and dip the bread into it, coating one side with butter; this is much quicker than spreading each slice with butter. Cut each slice in three and arrange half the bread over the base of the dish, butter side down. Cover with the dried fruit, lemon rind and half the sugar, and top with the rest of the bread, butter side uppermost. Sprinkle with the remaining sugar.

Blend the milk and eggs together and pour over the pudding. If time allows leave to stand for about an hour. If not bake at once in a preheated oven at 350°F, 180°C, gas mark 4, for about 40 minutes until puffy, a pale golden brown, and set.

Serves 6

Rhubarb Charlotte

Use the first of the rhubarb for this recipe.

Preparation time about 20 minutes
Cooking time about 40 minutes

1 lb (450 g) rhubarb, cut into short lengths
3 oz (75 g) demerara sugar
grated rind and juice of half a lemon
small sliced white loaf
4 oz (100 g) unsalted butter, melted

Put the rhubarb, 2 oz (50 g) of the sugar, and the lemon rind and juice in a saucepan and simmer gently for about 10 minutes or until the fruit is tender, pounding occasionally with a wooden spoon. Cool.

Trim the crusts from most of the bread and cut into long strips. Cover the base and sides of a greased 7-inch (17.5-cm) sandwich cake tin with some of the strips. Sprinkle with half the remaining sugar and pour over half the melted butter.

Spread the rhubarb mixture over and cover with the remaining bread strips, overlapping them. Pour over the melted butter, and sprinkle with the sugar. Bake in a hot oven at 400°F, 200°C, gas mark 6 for about 40 minutes or until golden brown. Serve hot with cream.

Serves 4 to 6

Butterscotch Saucy Pudding

When the main course is a bit sparse or it's a cold day, this goes down well.

Preparation time about 10 minutes
Cooking time about 45 minutes

Sponge
    2 oz (50 g) muscovado sugar
    2 oz (50 g) soft margarine
    1 egg
    3 oz (75 g) self-raising flour
    ½ level teaspoon baking powder
    2 to 3 tablespoons milk

Topping
    3 oz (75 g) butter
    5 oz (150 g) muscovado sugar
    4 tablespoons double cream

Heat the oven to 350°F, 180°C, gas mark 4, and lightly butter a 1-pint (600-ml) pie dish.

Put all the sponge ingredients in a bowl, beat well for about 2 minutes or until smooth, turn into the dish and smooth the top. Bake in the oven for about 45 minutes or until risen and golden brown.

Meanwhile prepare the topping sauce. Melt the butter in a saucepan, then add the sugar and cream and mix well. Bring to the boil and simmer gently for 3 minutes, stirring occasionally until thick and glossy. Pour over the sponge and place under a hot grill for about 2 minutes until the sauce begins to bubble, and serve at once.

Serves 4

Devon Mincement and Almond Pie

By no means a budget pudding, but rather special. Adding mincemeat to apples makes it spicy, go a long way, and very good with the almond topping.

Preparation time about 10 minutes
Cooking time about 45 to 60 minutes

8 oz (225 g) cooking apples, weighed after peeling, coring and slicing
6 oz (175 g) light soft brown sugar
8 oz (225 g) mincemeat
4 oz (100 g) soft margarine
4 oz (100 g) ground almonds
2 eggs, beaten

Heat the oven to 350°F, 180°C, gas mark 4.

Put the apples, 2 oz (50 g) of the sugar and mincemeat in a 2½-pint (1.4-litre) pie dish and mix well.

Put the remaining ingredients in a bowl and beat until well mixed. Spread over the apple mixture and then bake in the oven for about 45 to 60 minutes when the mixture will be firm to the touch and golden brown.

Serve hot with thin cream or custard.

Serves 6

Easy Apple and Apricot Pie

This is a quick pie, rather a cheat really, but a very good way to fill up a hungry family after a cold main course.

Preparation time about 10 minutes
Cooking time about 30 minutes

> *13-oz (385-g) can apple pie filling*
> *7½-oz (212-g) can apricots, drained*
> *juice of half a lemon*
> *about 6 oz (175 g) pastry crumbs (see page 179)*
> *about 4 teaspoons cold water*
> *a little granulated sugar*

Heat the oven to 425°F, 220°C, gas mark 7.

Put the apple pie filling in a bowl with the apricots and lemon juice and stir lightly until mixed. Turn into a 1-pint (600-ml) pie dish.

Put the pastry crumbs in a bowl and mix with sufficient cold water to make a firm dough. Roll out on a floured surface and use to cover the top of the pie. Brush with a little cold water or milk and then sprinkle with granulated sugar. Make two slits in the centre and then bake in the oven for about 30 minutes until the pastry is golden brown and the pie filling hot through.

Serve with vanilla ice cream.

Serves 4

Apple Brown Betty

To make a really special pudding, 5 minutes before serving pour over a little sherry and decorate with slices of a red-skinned eating apple. (*See picture facing page 32.*)

Preparation time about 15 minutes
Cooking time about 40 minutes

1½ to 2 lb (675 to 900 g) cooking apples
6 oz (175 g) fresh white breadcrumbs
2 oz (50 g) butter
4 oz (100 g) light muscovado sugar
¼ teaspoon grated nutmeg
grated rind and juice of half a lemon
4 oz (100 g) sultanas

Heat the oven to 375°F, 190°C, gas mark 5. Grease a 3-pint (1.7-litre) ovenproof dish.

Peel, core and slice the apples. Place a third of the breadcrumbs in the base of the dish and dot with butter then cover with half the apples.

Put the sugar, nutmeg, lemon rind and sultanas in a bowl and mix well. Sprinkle half this mixture over the apples and then add half the lemon juice. Repeat this layering, starting with the breadcrumbs dotted with butter, then the apples, sugar mixture and lemon juice and finishing with a final layer of breadcrumbs dotted with butter.

Bake in the oven for 40 minutes, when the breadcrumbs will be golden brown and crisp and the apples tender.

Serve hot with cream or custard.

Serves 6

Bramley Apple Cake

This is a regular Sunday lunch pudding. Either cook it under the joint or make it the day before and reheat it. Windfalls do well for this recipe. Serve it warm with cream. The left-overs are delicious for tea. I make it in about 7 minutes flat as I know the recipe off by heart – you'll find for the first time of making it will take about 10 minutes. Although the cooking time is longer, I just couldn't omit the recipe from the book!

Preparation time 10 minutes
Cooking time 1½ hours

5 oz (150 g) margarine, melted
2 large eggs
8 oz (225 g) caster sugar
1 teaspoon almond essence
1 level teaspoon baking powder
8 oz (225 g) self-raising flour
12 oz (350 g) Bramleys, sliced (weighed after preparation)
1 oz (25 g) flaked almonds
sprinkling of demerara sugar

Heat oven to 325°F, 160°C, gas mark 3. Grease a loose-bottomed 8-inch (20-cm) cake tin.

Put all ingredients, except apples, almonds and demerara sugar, in a mixing bowl. Mix well until smooth. Spread half this mixture over the base of the tin. Spoon over prepared apple. Dot with rough teaspoons of the remaining mixture, sprinkle with almonds and demerara sugar.

Bake for about 1½ hours until pale golden and shrinking away from the sides of the tin. Cool slightly, lift out of the tin and serve with cream or ice cream.

Serves 8

Apple Fritters

This batter can also be used to coat bananas, when it is best to use slightly under-ripe fruit. (*See picture facing page 32.*)

Preparation time about 10 minutes
Cooking time about 3 to 4 minutes

1 lb (450 g) cooking apples
4 oz (100 g) plain flour
1 egg, separated
¼ pint (150 ml) milk
deep fat or oil for frying
caster sugar
cinnamon

Peel and quarter the apples and remove the cores. If the apples are very large cut the quarters in half. (If liked the apples could be peeled and cut across in rings.)

Put the flour in a bowl and make a well in the centre. Blend the egg yolk with the milk and then add to the flour to make a smooth thick batter. Whisk the egg white until stiff and then fold into the batter.

Heat the oil or fat in a large pan, dip the fruit into the batter, one piece at a time, and then fry until golden brown. Lift out with a slotted spoon and drain on kitchen paper. Toss in a mixture of caster sugar with a little cinnamon added and then serve at once with a jug of thin cream.

Serves 4

Old English Baked Apples

Serve these when you have the oven on for the main course. Serve with lots of cream or a large scoop of vanilla ice cream.

Preparation time about 5 minutes
Cooking time about 35 to 40 minutes

4 large cooking apples
2 oz (50 g) light soft brown sugar
2 oz (50 g) butter
2 tablespoons water

Heat the oven to 350°F, 180°C, gas mark 4.

Wipe the apples and remove the cores, using a sharp knife or corer, and make a slit around the centre of each apple. Place in an oven-proof dish and fill the centres with sugar, put a knob of butter on top of each, and pour round the water.

Bake in the oven for about 35 to 40 minutes or until the apples are soft and puffy (the time can vary according to the size and variety of apples). The water with the sugar and butter in the apples will make a sauce to spoon over them.

Serve hot.

Serves 4

Mincemeat Apples

Instead of sugar fill the centres with mincemeat and then proceed as above.

Jammy Apples

Instead of sugar fill the centres with jam – raspberry or plum are good. No need to top with butter.

Orange Apples

Cream the sugar with the butter and beat in the rind of a small orange. Use to fill the centres of the apples and, instead of water, use the juice of the orange.

Honey Baked Apples

Instead of sugar fill the centres with a mixture of honey and sultanas. Allow a heaped tablespoon honey and a teaspoonful of sultanas to each apple. Omit the water and serve with cream or a little extra melted honey.

Crispy Oat Crumble

Use any fruit that is in season for this recipe, or a combination of fruits.

Preparation time about 10 minutes
Cooking time about 45 minutes

> *3 oz (75 g) plain flour*
> *3 oz (75 g) soft margarine*
> *3 oz (75 g) rolled oats*
> *2 oz (50 g) demerara sugar*
> *1½ lb (675 g) rhubarb*
> *4 oz (100 g) caster sugar*
> *2 tablespoons water*

Heat the oven to 400°F, 200°C, gas mark 6.

Put the flour in a bowl, add the margarine cut in small pieces and rub in with the fingertips until the mixture resembles breadcrumbs. Stir in the oats and demerara sugar.

Cut the rhubarb into 1-inch (2.5-cm) lengths and put into a 1¾-pint (1-litre) pie dish with the caster sugar and water. Pile the crumble on top so that it completely covers the rhubarb and bake in the oven for about 45 minutes until the fruit is tender and the crumble golden brown.

Serve hot with custard and a little extra demerara sugar if liked.

Serves 4

Wholewheat Crumble
Instead of plain flour use wholewheat flour and add ½ teaspoon of cinnamon. This mixture is very good with gooseberries and apples.

Right: Apple Brown Betty (page 27) and Apple and Banana Fritters (page 29).

Greengage Eves Pudding

Lovely on a cold day.

Preparation time about 5 minutes
Cooking time about 40 minutes

1¼-lb (550-g) can greengages or plums
4 oz (100 g) soft margarine
3 oz (75 g) caster sugar
2 eggs, beaten
6 oz (175 g) self-raising flour
1 level teaspoon baking powder
2 tablespoons milk
1 tablespoon demerara sugar

Heat the oven to 375°F, 190°C, gas mark 5.

Drain the greengages and place in a 2-pint (a good litre) ovenproof dish with just 3 tablespoons of their juice.

Put all the remaining ingredients except the demerara sugar into a bowl and beat well for about 2 minutes until well blended.

Spread the mixture over the top of the greengages and smooth the top. Sprinkle with the demerara sugar and bake in the oven for about 40 minutes or until the sponge is well risen and golden brown and will spring back when lightly pressed with a finger.

Serves 4 to 6

Left: Butterscotch Fudge Cake (page 40).

Chocolate Soufflé

If you can make a good white sauce you can easily make a good soufflé. If time is short make individual ones as they cook in half the time.

Preparation time about 15 minutes
Cooking time about 40 minutes

> *3.5-oz (100-g) bar plain chocolate*
> *2 tablespoons water*
> *½ pint (300 ml) milk*
> *1½ oz (40 g) butter*
> *1½ oz (40 g) flour*
> *¼ teaspoon vanilla essence*
> *4 large eggs*
> *2 oz (50 g) caster sugar*
> *a little icing sugar*

Heat the oven to 375°F, 190°C, gas mark 5, and place a baking sheet in it. Butter a 2-pint (a good litre) soufflé dish.

Break the chocolate into small pieces, put in a saucepan with the water and 2 tablespoons milk, and stir over a low heat until the chocolate has melted. Add the remaining milk, bring to the boil, then remove from the heat.

Melt the butter in a small pan, stir in the flour and cook for 2 minutes without browning. Remove from the heat and stir in the hot milk, return to the heat and bring to the boil, stirring until thickened. Add the vanilla essence and then leave to cool.

Separate the eggs and beat the yolks one at a time into the chocolate sauce and then sprinkle on the caster sugar. Whisk the egg whites using a rotary hand or electric whisk until they are stiff but not dry. Stir 1 tablespoon into the chocolate mixture and then carefully fold in the remainder. Pour into the dish, run a teaspoon around the edge and bake on the hot baking sheet in the centre of the oven for 40 minutes.

Sprinkle with icing sugar and serve at once with whipped cream.

Serves 4

Choose any of the following flavourings, instead of the chocolate and 2 tablespoons of water, and add to the mixture before the egg yolks.

Lemon Soufflé

Add the finely grated rind of 2 small lemons and the juice of half a lemon to the mixture with a spoonful of lemon curd. Leave out the vanilla essence and increase the caster sugar to 3 oz (75 g).

Orange Soufflé

Add the finely grated rind of 2 small oranges and the juice of half an orange to the mixture. Leave out the vanilla essence and increase the caster sugar to 3 oz (75 g). Serve with cream to which a little fresh orange juice has been added.

Coffee Soufflé

Add 2 to 3 tablespoons coffee essence to the milk and leave out the vanilla essence.

Pots de Crème

Always a firm favourite, these baked egg custards are easy to prepare. (*Illustrated on the jacket.*)

Preparation time about 5 minutes
Cooking time about 25 to 30 minutes

4 eggs
1 oz (25 g) caster sugar
1 pint (600 ml) milk
a little grated nutmeg
whipped cream
toasted almonds or grated chocolate

Heat the oven to 325°F, 160°C, gas mark 3. Butter 6 individual ovenproof dishes or ramekins.

Beat eggs and sugar together. Heat the milk to just below boiling and gradually whisk into the egg mixture. Strain into the dishes and stand in a baking tin with warm water to come half-way up the sides. Sprinkle each dish with a little nutmeg.

Bake in the oven for about 25 to 30 minutes until firm, then remove from the oven and leave to cool. Chill in the refrigerator.

When required top each dish with a swirl of whipped cream and sprinkle with toasted almonds, or a little grated chocolate if liked.

Serves 6

Orange Pots de Crème

Add the grated rind of 1 or 2 oranges to the basic mixture. I usually find 1 large orange will give sufficient flavour. Bake as above but omit the nutmeg and almonds and serve sprinkled with grated chocolate.

MAKE A DAY AHEAD

Peace of mind is what we all hope for. Probably nobody needs it more than the busy housewife with a demanding, hungry family to feed, the hostess with a dinner party ahead of her and little time to prepare for it. Anything that cuts down last-minute work is welcome. One ready-made course can give you an enormous sense of relief when the time comes to devote yourself to the rest of the meal.

A pudding prepared the day before is the cook's friend. The knowledge that you have a fruit cheesecake, perhaps, or a raspberry pavlova, a special fruit salad, waiting in the fridge to be produced at the end of dinner can do an enormous amount for your confidence and can only enhance your fame as a relaxed hostess.

There are recipes here for every occasion from the gala dinner to the family supper. None in itself takes long to make. All are improved by a night's rest in the fridge or freezer, which gives jellies time to set, fruits to blend their flavours, creams to chill.

Real Crème Brûlée

Expensive to make but quick and a real luxury. Just sprinkle with demerara sugar, slip under the grill and brown a couple of hours before serving, then chill.

Preparation time about 5 minutes
Cooking time about 1 hour

3 eggs
¾ pint (450 ml) single cream
1½ oz (40 g) caster sugar
a few drops of vanilla essence
2 to 3 oz (50 to 75 g) demerara sugar

Heat the oven to 300°F, 150°C, gas mark 2.

Blend the eggs, cream, caster sugar and vanilla essence together and turn into an ovenproof dish. Stand in a meat tin containing 1 inch (2.5 cm) hot water and bake in the oven for about 1 hour or until just firm. Remove from the oven and cool, then leave in the refrigerator overnight.

A couple of hours before serving, sprinkle the top with demerara sugar and brown under a hot grill for 3 to 4 minutes until sugar has melted and become crisp. Leave to cool and then serve.

Serves 4

Small Caramel Custards

Leave in the ramekin dishes or cups until the last moment before turning out, otherwise the caramel topping loses its shine and colour. Serve very cold. Make a large crème caramel in a 1¾-pint (1-litre) soufflé dish and bake in the oven for about 1½ hours.

Preparation time about 10 minutes
Cooking time about 45 to 60 minutes

3 oz (75 g) granulated sugar
3 tablespoons water
5 eggs
2 oz (50 g) caster sugar
a few drops of vanilla essence
1¼ pints (750 ml) milk

Heat the oven to 300°F, 150°C, gas mark 2.

To make the caramel, put the granulated sugar and water in a heavy saucepan and dissolve over a low heat. Bring to the boil and boil until the syrup is a pale golden brown. Remove from the heat and quickly pour into 6 small ramekins or dishes.

For the crème, mix the eggs, caster sugar and vanilla essence together. Warm the milk in a saucepan over a low heat until it is hand hot, then pour it onto the egg mixture, stirring constantly.

Butter the sides of the ramekins above the caramel. Strain the custard into the ramekins, and place in a roasting tin half filled with hot water. Bake in the oven for about 45 to 60 minutes or until a knife inserted in the centre comes out clean. Remove from the oven and leave to completely cool and set for at least 12 hours or overnight. Turn out onto individual dishes.

Serves 6

Butterscotch Fudge Cake

I like to make this a day ahead and leave overnight in the refrigerator. But you can make it at the beginning of the day and leave for about 3 hours to set. (*See picture facing page 33.*)

Preparation time about 10 to 12 minutes

6 oz (175 g) unsalted butter
6 tablespoons golden syrup
4 oz (100 g) glacé cherries, chopped
8 oz (225 g) mixed dried fruit
4 oz (100 g) mixed nuts, roughly chopped
8 oz (225 g) wheatmeal biscuits

To decorate
a little whipped cream
glacé cherries

Place the butter and syrup in a heavy pan and place over a gentle heat until the butter has melted, then boil for 2 to 3 minutes, stirring constantly. Leave to cool for a few minutes.

Place all the fruits and nuts in a large bowl. Crush half the biscuits and crumble the other half and add to the fruit and nuts. Pour over the butterscotch sauce and stir well until evenly coated. Spoon the mixture into an 8-inch (20-cm) loose based cake tin and leave to set in the refrigerator.

When set turn out, place on a serving dish and decorate with swirls of cream and glacé cherries.

Makes about 10 to 12 slices

Traditional
Summer Pudding

This is a recipe I am including because it really is simple and quick to make, and so delicious. I often double the recipe and freeze one pudding. Vary the fruits according to what is available. (*Illustrated on the jacket.*)

Preparation time about 15 minutes

6 to 8 large, fairly thin slices white bread with the crusts removed
8 oz (225 g) rhubarb
8 oz (225 g) blackcurrants
8 oz (225 g) granulated sugar
6 tablespoons water
8 oz (225 g) small strawberries
8 oz (225 g) raspberries

Put one slice of bread on one side for the top, and use the remainder to line the base and sides of a 2-pint (a good litre) basin, or round fairly shallow dish.

Put the rhubarb, cut in ½-inch (1.25-cm) slices, and blackcurrants into a saucepan, and add the sugar and water. Bring to the boil and simmer for a few minutes until barely tender, stirring. Add the strawberries and raspberries and cook for a further minute.

Turn into the dish, place the slice of bread on top and bend over the tops of the sliced bread at the sides towards the centre. Place a saucer on top, pressing down a little until the juices rise to the top of the basin or dish.

Leave to soak until cold and then put in the refrigerator overnight. Turn out just before serving, with lots of thick cream.

Serves 4 to 6

Rhubarb Fool

This is a quick and easy pudding and few people even guess that it is rhubarb.

Preparation time about 10 minutes
Cooking time about 15 minutes

    1½ lb (675 g) rhubarb
    4 tablespoons sugar
    6 tablespoons water
    ½ pint (300 ml) double cream

Wash and cut the rhubarb into 1-inch (2.5-cm) lengths. Put in a saucepan with the sugar and water and simmer gently until tender about 15 minutes. Rub the rhubarb through a sieve or reduce to a purée in a blender or processor, and leave to cool.

Whisk the cream until it forms soft peaks and then fold in the purée. Pour into a serving dish and then leave in the refrigerator overnight to chill thoroughly.

Serves 4 to 6

Figgy Cream

Canned figs are expensive but delicious. Serve very cold.

Preparation time about 10 minutes

15-oz (425-g) can of figs
½ pint (300 ml) whipping cream
½ pint (300 ml) natural yogurt
dark soft brown sugar

Drain the figs, then roughly chop, place in a bowl and add sufficient syrup to make them just moist.

Lightly whip the cream until it forms soft peaks and then stir in the yogurt. Place a spoonful of the cream and yogurt mixture in the base of 4 individual glass dishes, then divide the figs equally between the glasses. Top with the remaining cream mixture and smooth flat.

Sprinkle the dishes with a ¼ inch (6 mm) layer of sugar. Leave in the refrigerator for several hours or overnight. When ready to serve, sprinkle with more sugar.

Serves 4

Fruit Passion

So easy and very good, this pudding consists of a fruit layer topped with a blend of yogurt and cream, with a layer of dark brown sugar which becomes a rich syrup overnight.

Preparation time about 10 minutes

raspberries or strawberries
½ pint (300 ml) whipping cream
½ pint (300 ml) plain yogurt
dark soft brown sugar

Take 4 individual glasses and put a few raspberries or sliced strawberries on the base of each, or you could use a combination.

Lightly whip the cream and blend with the yogurt. Put the mixture on top of the fruit. Sprinkle the top of each glass with a ¼-inch (6-mm) thick layer of sugar. Leave overnight in the refrigerator.

Sprinkle with a little extra sugar just before serving.

Serves 4

Hazelnut Meringue

This is a very versatile pudding. You can serve it on its own, or with peaches in brandy (see page 111), a large bowl of fresh strawberries or raspberries, and a big bowl of whipped cream. The children like it best served with chocolate toffee sauce (see page 153).

Preparation time about 15 minutes
Cooking time about 40 minutes

4 oz (100 g) shelled and skinned hazelnuts
4 egg whites
8 oz (225 g) caster sugar
1 teaspoon vinegar
¼ pint (150 ml) whipping cream
icing sugar

Heat the oven to 350°F, 180°C, gas mark 4. Lightly brush the insides of 2 × 8-inch (20-cm) sponge cake tins with oil, line with greaseproof paper, and brush again with oil.

Put the hazelnuts in a blender and chop finely, spread on a baking tray and put in the oven for about 8 to 10 minutes until a pale golden brown. Remove and tip onto a plate to quickly cool.

Meanwhile whisk the egg whites with an electric whisk until stiff and then whisk in the caster sugar a teaspoonful at a time, adding the vinegar with the last spoonful of sugar. Carefully fold in the hazelnuts using a metal spoon.

Divide the mixture evenly between the cake tins and smooth the tops. Bake in the oven for 40 minutes, then turn off the heat and leave to cool. Remove from the tins and peel off the paper.

Whisk the cream until thick and sandwich the meringues together. Place on a serving dish and then dredge with icing sugar. Leave to stand for about 1 hour before serving.

Serves 8 to 10

Raspberry Pavlova

Quicker to cook than meringue, the middle should be soft and squidgy.

Preparation time about 10 minutes
Cooking time about 1 hour

   3 egg whites
   6 oz (175 g) caster sugar
   1 teaspoon vinegar
   1 level teaspoon cornflour
   ½ pint (300 ml) whipping or double cream, whipped
   8 oz (225 g) raspberries

Lay a sheet of silicone paper (non-stick vegetable parchment) on a baking tray and mark an 8-inch (20-cm) circle on it. Heat the oven to 325°F, 160°C, gas mark 3.

Whisk the egg whites with a hand rotary or electric whisk until stiff, then whisk in the sugar a spoonful at a time. Blend the vinegar with the cornflour and whisk into the egg whites with the last spoonful of sugar. Spread the meringue out to cover the circle on a baking tray, building up the sides so that they are higher than the centre.

Put in the centre of the oven, turn the heat down to 300°F, 150°C, gas mark 2 and bake for 1 hour. The pavlova will be a pale creamy colour rather than white. Turn the oven off and leave the pavlova to become quite cold in the oven. Remove from the baking tray and place on a serving dish.

Fold the cream and raspberries together and pile into the centre of the pavlova. If time allows leave to stand for an hour before serving.

Serves 6 to 8

Mixed Fruit Pavlova

Try filling with a combination of whipped cream, pears and small grapes or sliced bananas and kiwi fruit.

Kiwi and Strawberry Pavlova *(See picture facing page 64.)*

Peel and slice 3 kiwi fruits and halve 4 to 6 oz (100 to 175 g) strawberries. Fold half the fruit into the whipped cream, pile into the centre of the pavlova, and decorate with the remaining fruit.

Midsummer Fruit Jelly

Most people like jelly, especially when it is bursting with fruits. Make it at the height of the season in summer, and it's essential you make it in a pretty shallow glass bowl to give the best effect.

Preparation time about 5 minutes

1 packet raspberry jelly
boiling water
strawberries
raspberries
blackcurrants
redcurrants

Make up the raspberry jelly as directed on the packet with the boiling water and leave on one side to cool, but not set.

Carefully arrange the fruit in lines or in circles in a shallow glass dish. If the strawberries are large cut in half, or use small whole ones. Spoon over the jelly and leave undisturbed in a cool place to set, preferably overnight.

Serves 4 to 6

Raspberry and Port Jelly

If you have frozen raspberries, use them in preference to a can, and in both cases the liquid should be 1 pint (600 ml).

Preparation time about 5 minutes

1 packet lemon jelly
15-oz (425-g) can of raspberries
about ¼ pint (150 ml) port

Dampen a generous 1-pint (600-ml) jelly mould and leave to drain.

Break the jelly into pieces, put in a measure and make up to ½ pint (300 ml) with boiling water. Stir until dissolved. Drain the syrup from the raspberries and add to the jelly with the port. Stir until blended and, if necessary, add a little extra water to make up to 1 pint (600 ml).

Stir in the raspberries and then turn into the mould. Leave to cool and then set in the refrigerator overnight. Dip the mould into hot water for about 10 to 15 seconds, cover with a plate and turn out. Serve with whipped cream.

Serves 4

Brandied Raspberries

If you have raspberries from the garden that were picked on a wet day, perhaps, or were the last of the season, this is a very good way of serving them. Goes well with vanilla ice cream.

Preparation time about 10 minutes

> 12 oz (350 g) granulated sugar
> ¾ pint (450 ml) water
> 2 tablespoons arrowroot
> 2 tablespoons brandy
> 1 lb (450 g) frozen raspberries

Place the sugar in a saucepan with the water and heat gently until the sugar has dissolved and then boil for 2 to 3 minutes. Remove the pan from the heat.

Blend the arrowroot with the brandy, add a little of the syrup, mix well and then return to the saucepan. Bring to the boil, stirring, until the syrup has thickened slightly. Remove from the heat and leave to cool slightly, then stir in the raspberries.

Turn into a serving dish and leave in a cool place until required.

Serves 4 to 6

Loganberry Cream

It is essential to sieve the loganberries first as the pips spoil the smoothness.

Preparation time about 15 minutes

15-oz (425-g) can loganberries
1 packet raspberry jelly
¼ pint (150 ml) double cream
¼ pint (150 ml) single cream

Strain the juice from the loganberries into a measure and make up to ½ pint (300 ml) with water. Heat the juice to boiling point in a small pan, remove from the heat and then add the jelly broken in small pieces and stir until dissolved. Pour into a bowl and leave in a cool place until it begins to thicken.

Whisk the two creams together until thick and they form soft peaks.

Sieve the loganberries, keeping a few whole ones for decoration. Fold the sieved loganberries into the jelly with the cream and divide between 4 individual glasses or dishes and leave in a cool place to set. Decorate with the whole loganberries just before serving.

Serves 4

Lemon Mallow Mousse

This is a nice refreshing mousse with small pieces of marshmallow folded through it.

Preparation time about 20 minutes

>   2 oz (50 g) white marshmallows
>   4 eggs
>   4 oz (100 g) caster sugar
>   2 lemons
>   ½ oz (12.5 g) gelatine
>   3 tablespoons cold water
>   ¼ pint (150 ml) double cream, lightly whipped

Snip each marshmallow into about 6 pieces with a pair of scissors. Separate the eggs, place the yolks in a bowl with the sugar, and beat well until blended and creamy. Put the egg whites in a large bowl ready for whisking. Grate the rind and squeeze the juice from the lemons and add to the yolks.

Put the gelatine and water in a small bowl or cup. Stand for 3 minutes until it becomes a sponge, then stand in a pan of simmering water and allow the gelatine to dissolve. Cool slightly and add to the yolk and lemon mixture. Leave to cool and start to thicken, but do not allow to set.

Whisk the egg whites with a rotary or electric hand whisk until stiff. Fold the cream and marshmallows into the lemon mixture and finally fold in the egg whites. Turn into a 2-pint (a good litre) glass serving dish and leave to set for at least 4 hours. If liked the top may be decorated with a few whole marshmallows.

Serves 4 to 6

Lemon Syllabub

This is a simple rich sweet that I like to serve with shortbread biscuits (page 188). (*See picture facing page 65.*)

Preparation time about 5 minutes

½ pint (300 ml) double cream
finely grated rind and juice of 1 lemon
1 tablespoon brandy
1 tablespoon sherry
2 oz (50 g) caster sugar

Place all the ingredients together in a bowl and whisk until light but not thick.

Turn into 4 small glasses or syllabub cups and leave in the refrigerator until required.

Serves 4

Lemon Chiffon Pie

This pie has a sharp lemon filling that goes well with the biscuit crust.

Preparation time about 15 minutes
Cooking time about 20 minutes

3 oz (75 g) butter
6 oz (175 g) digestive biscuits, crushed
2 oz (50 g) demerara sugar

Filling
grated rind and juice of 2 large lemons
3 oz (75 g) caster sugar
2 level tablespoons cornflour
2 large eggs, separated
2 tablespoons home-made lemon curd or bought lemon cheese

To make the crust, melt the butter in a saucepan and then add the biscuit crumbs and sugar. Mix very well and line a 9-inch (22.5-cm) flan tin that does not have a loose base. Put in the refrigerator to chill. Heat the oven to 400°F, 200°C, gas mark 6.

Now make the filling. Place the lemon juice and rind in a measure and make up to ½ pint (300 ml) with water. In a bowl mix the sugar and cornflour with a little of the lemon juice to make a paste, then add the egg yolks. Place the remaining lemon juice mixture in a saucepan and bring to the boil, pour onto the paste, mix well and then return to the pan and bring to the boil, stirring until thickened. Remove from the heat and stir in the lemon curd. Leave to cool slightly.

Whisk the egg whites until stiff and then fold into the lemon custard. Turn into the flan case and bake in the oven for about 20 minutes until lightly brown on top. Remove, leave to cool and then chill thoroughly before serving.

Serves 6

Sharp Grapefruit Cheesecake

Easy to make and very refreshing. Decorate with any fresh fruit – strawberries or small bunches of fresh redcurrants look good. Make an orange cheesecake in exactly the same way, using a can of frozen concentrated unsweetened *orange* juice.

Preparation time about 20 minutes

> *½ oz (12.5 g) gelatine or one packet*
> *3 tablespoons cold water*
> *1 lb (450 g) rich cream cheese*
> *6-oz (175-g) can frozen concentrated unsweetened grapefruit juice,*
>   *thawed*
> *3 oz (75 g) caster sugar*
> *½ pint (300 ml) whipping cream*
> *4 oz (100 g) digestive biscuits*
> *2 oz (50 g) butter*
> *1 oz (25 g) demerara sugar*
> *black and white grapes, strawberries, or redcurrants to decorate*

Place the gelatine in a small basin with cold water and leave to stand for 3 minutes. Then place the basin in a pan of simmering water and leave until the gelatine has dissolved and become clear. Remove from heat and cool.

Cream the cheese until soft and gradually beat in the grapefruit juice and caster sugar. Stir in the cooled gelatine. Whisk the cream until it is thick but not stiff and fold into the cheese mixture. Turn into a lightly oiled 8-inch (20-cm) cake tin with a circle of greaseproof paper in the bottom. Place in the refrigerator.

Crush the biscuits finely. Melt the butter in a pan and stir in the biscuit crumbs and demerara sugar. Press over the cheesecake and leave in the refrigerator overnight. Turn out onto a serving dish and remove the paper. Decorate with fruit.

Serves 8

American Cheesecake

This makes the first of the year's strawberries look rather special.

Preparation time about 10 minutes

Flan case
  3 oz (75 g) butter
  1½ oz (40 g) demerara sugar
  6 oz (175 g) digestive biscuits, crushed

Filling
  4 oz (100 g) cream cheese
  juice of 1½ lemons
  *½ pint (300 ml) double cream, lightly whipped with a little sugar to
    taste*
  6 strawberries

For the flan case, melt the butter in a saucepan, stir in the sugar and crushed biscuits and mix thoroughly. Press over the base and sides of an 8-inch (20-cm) flan ring on a plate or a loose bottomed flan tin, using a metal spoon.

For the filling, cream the cheese with the lemon juice and a little of the whipped cream until soft and then fold in the remaining cream. Turn into the flan case and leave in a cool place to set. Hull the strawberries and arrange on top.

Serves 6

RICH AND SPECIAL

These are the special occasion ones, the frankly extravagant ones, full of cream and booze and party spirit and no expense spared. After all, you don't entertain every day, so make the most of it when you do and give your guests something to remember.

These recipes admittedly take longer than some of the others. But then you usually know in advance when you are going to have a dinner party, so you can prepare the puddings the day before and with that off your mind you can concentrate on the other courses, secure in the knowledge that the final one is waiting ready in the fridge.

If there is an emergency and you want something really delicious at a moment's notice, you can make an impressive zabaglione literally in minutes. I will guarantee that your reputation as a cook won't suffer.

Peach and Raspberry Brûlée

It is important to use a shallow ovenproof dish that will easily fit under the grill.

Preparation time about 10 minutes
Cooking time about 3 to 4 minutes

15-oz (425-g) can white peaches
8 oz (225 g) raspberries
a little icing sugar
3 to 4 tablespoons brandy or white rum
½ pint (300 ml) double cream
light soft brown sugar

Drain the peaches, cut into equal sized pieces and place in a shallow ovenproof dish about 2 pint (1 litre) capacity. Add the raspberries and sprinkle with a little icing sugar. Sprinkle over the brandy or rum, and chill until required.

Lightly whip the cream until it just forms soft peaks and spread over the top of the fruit. Scatter the sugar quite thickly over the top of the cream.

Place under a hot grill until the sugar begins to darken and goes a deep golden brown. Serve at once.

Serves 6

Zabaglione

This rich luxurious dessert is always a treat. It is best served at once as it soon begins to separate out. Serve with sweet biscuits such as *langues de chat* or sponge fingers (see page 182). If making for children use 6 tablespoons of lemon juice instead of the Marsala.

Preparation time about 12 minutes

> *6 tablespoons Marsala, Madeira or sweet sherry*
> *4 oz (100 g) caster sugar*
> *4 egg yolks*

Stand a heatproof glass bowl over a pan of simmering water. Measure the Marsala and sugar into the bowl and leave to get really warm, but not hot.

Add the egg yolks and begin whisking at once on a high speed with a rotary or electric hand whisk. Continue whisking for about 5 minutes until the mixture is light and foamy. Pour into 4 large glasses and serve at once.

Serves 4

Royal Pancakes

Pancakes are always popular and not just on Shrove Tuesday! Keep a few ready-made in the freezer, interleaved with greaseproof paper.

Preparation time about 12 minutes

Brandy butter
  8 oz (225 g) unsalted butter, softened
  8 oz (225 g) icing sugar
  6 tablespoons brandy
  about 8 to 10 pancakes (see page 186)

For the brandy butter, place the butter in a bowl and beat well until soft. Gradually sieve in the icing sugar and continue beating until light and fluffy. Add the brandy and beat well to mix. Put in the refrigerator to harden.

Make the pancakes and place on a piece of sugared paper. Place a spoonful of the brandy butter on each pancake, roll up and serve at once on a hot serving dish.

Serves 4 to 5

Griestorte with Pineapple and Ginger

Providing that you have a small electric hand mixer or strong right arm and whisk this is very quick to make.

Preparation time about 15 minutes
Cooking time about 30 minutes

3 eggs, separated
4 oz (100 g) caster sugar
½ teaspoon almond essence
2 oz (50 g) semolina
½ oz (15 g) ground almonds

Filling
8-oz (227-g) can of pineapple
¼ pint (150 ml) double cream
a little preserved stem ginger, chopped

Heat the oven to 350°F, 180°C, gas mark 4. Grease and line an 8-inch (20-cm) round cake tin with greased greaseproof paper and dust with flour.

Put the egg yolks and sugar in a heatproof bowl over a pan of hot water and whisk until the mixture is pale and thick. Remove from the heat. Fold in the almond essence, semolina and ground almonds.

Whisk the egg whites until they form soft peaks and then fold into the mixture. Turn into the cake tin and bake in the oven for about 30 minutes or until the cake is well risen and pale golden brown. Turn out, remove the paper and leave to cool on a wire rack. Split the cake in half horizontally.

For the filling, drain the pineapple thoroughly and then chop finely. Whisk the cream until thick and then stir in the pineapple and a little finely chopped stem ginger. Use the cream mixture to sandwich the cake together. Place on a serving dish and if liked sprinkle with sugar.

Serves 8

Chocolate Hazelnut Meringue Gâteau

A dessert cake for a party that serves 12 and tastes glorious. If you haven't any small meringues to decorate the top, more's the pity, because it does make it look tremendous. (*Illustrated on the jacket.*)

Preparation time about 20 minutes

Cake
> *46 sponge finger biscuits*
> *about ½ pint (300 ml) strong black coffee*
> *6 tablespoons sherry or Tia Maria*

Filling
> *1½ oz (40 g) cocoa*
> *4 tablespoons hot water*
> *3 oz (75 g) butter*
> *3 oz (75 g) icing sugar, sieved*
> *1 egg*
> *2 to 3 oz (50 to 75 g) hazelnuts, chopped*

Decoration
> *½ pint (300 ml) double cream*
> *1 oz (25 g) icing sugar*
> *approximately 12 small meringues (see page 185)*
> *a square of chocolate, grated*
> *toasted hazelnuts*

Line an 8- or 9-inch (20- or 22.5-cm) round cake tin with a circle of greaseproof paper.

Dip each sponge finger into a mixture of coffee and sherry or Tia Maria in a shallow dish. Use the fingers to line the bottom of the tin, cutting some to fit, taking care not to let them get too soft. Use about one-third.

To prepare the filling, put the cocoa and water in a bowl and stir until smooth. Beat in the butter and icing sugar with the egg and nuts. Spread half of this over the sponge fingers in the tin. Cover with more sponge fingers, the rest of the filling and then a final layer of sponge fingers.

Leave for several hours in the refrigerator (it will keep for several days). Turn out into a flat serving dish and remove the paper.

Whisk the cream until thick and add the icing sugar. Coat the top and sides of the cake with two-thirds of the cream and press the meringues around the sides. Decorate the top with grated chocolate and hazelnuts and with piped swirls of cream.

Serves 12

Black Cherry Gâteau

This is a delicious way to serve a plain chocolate sponge.

Preparation time about 10 to 15 minutes

2 basic chocolate sponges (see page 180)
15-oz (420-g) can pitted black cherries
1¹/₂ level tablespoons cornflour
¹/₂ pint (300 ml) double cream
about 2 oz (50 g) coarsely grated chocolate

Split each sponge in half horizontally.

Drain the can of cherries and save the juice. Place the cornflour in a small saucepan and stir in the cherry juice, place over a moderate heat and bring to the boil, stirring until the sauce has thickened. Simmer for 2 minutes. Remove the pan from the heat and stir in the cherries. Leave to cool.

Sandwich the layers of cake together with the cherry sauce. Whisk the cream until thick and then spread a little around the sides of the cake and coat with some of the grated chocolate. Place the cake on a serving plate and spread or pipe the remaining cream over the top of the cake (it looks good if piped in rosettes).

Sprinkle with the remaining chocolate and leave in a cool place until required.

Serves 6 to 8

Right: Kiwi and Strawberry Pavlova (page 47).

Lemon Cheesecake

Decorate the top of this cheesecake with fruits that are in season – grapes, sliced kiwi fruit, strawberries or sugared lemon slices.

Preparation time about 15 minutes

3 oz (75 g) digestive biscuits
1½ oz (40 g) butter
1 oz (25 g) demerara sugar
8 oz (225 g) cream cheese
large can of condensed milk
grated rind and juice of 3 lemons
¼ pint (150 ml) soured cream
fresh seasonal fruit to decorate

Place the biscuits in a polythene bag and crush with a rolling pin. Melt the butter in a small saucepan, add the sugar and biscuits and mix well. Turn into an 8-inch (20-cm) loose bottomed cake tin and press firmly onto the base with the back of a spoon.

Put the cream cheese into a bowl and cream well until soft, then beat in the condensed milk until smooth. Mix in the lemon juice and rind. Pour over the biscuit base, smooth, and leave in the refrigerator until set.

Loosen the sides of the tin, press up the base and lift onto a flat dish. Spread the top of the cheesecake with soured cream and then decorate with fruit.

Serves 6 to 8

Left: Lemon Syllabub (page 53), Shortbread Fingers (page 188) and Honey and Banana Pancakes (page 91).

Mont Blanc

A very rich and special pudding, made to look like a mountain.

Preparation time about 45 minutes
Cooking time about 25 to 30 minutes

Base
   2 oz (50 g) caster sugar
   2 oz (50 g) soft margarine
   2 oz (50 g) self-raising flour
   1 egg
   ½ level teaspoon baking powder

Filling
   2 oz (50 g) granulated sugar
   4 tablespoons water
   2 oz (50 g) soft butter, unsalted is best
   15½-oz (439-g) can unsweetened chestnut purée
   ½ pint (300 ml) double cream, whipped until thick
   2 to 3 tablespoons brandy

Heat the oven to 350°F, 180°C, gas mark 4, and grease and flour a 1-pint (600-ml) pudding basin.

Put all the ingredients for the base in a bowl and beat well until mixed, turn into the basin and bake in the oven for about 25 minutes or until risen and golden brown. Leave to cool on a wire rack.

To make the filling, place the sugar and water in a small saucepan and heat gently until the sugar has dissolved, then boil for a minute. Stir into the chestnut purée in a bowl with the butter, and mix thoroughly. Beat in about 3 tablespoons whipped cream.

Place the sponge base on a serving dish and pour over the brandy. Pile the chestnut mixture on top of the sponge base in a dome and cover with the cream, using a round ended knife so that the cream looks like snow on a mountain.

Serves 8

Chestnut Delight

Perfect for a special dinner party or buffet supper, this pudding is very rich, so serve it in thin slices.

Preparation time about 25 to 30 minutes

2 tablespoons sherry
2 tablespoons water
about 28 sponge fingers

Filling
3½-oz (100-g) bar of plain chocolate
4 oz (100 g) unsalted butter, softened
6 oz (175 g) caster sugar
15½-oz (439-g) can unsweetened chestnut purée

Decoration
¼ pint (150 ml) whipping cream, whipped
a little grated chocolate

Put the sherry and water in a flat dish. Take a 2-lb (900-g) loaf tin. Dip the unsugared side of about half the sponge fingers quickly in the sherry mixture and cover the base of the loaf tin with them, sugar side down. Cut the remaining biscuits in half, dip the unsugared side in sherry and then stand them around the sides of the tin, sugar side out.

Now make the filling. Break the chocolate into pieces, put in a bowl and stand over a pan of gently simmering water to melt. Cream the butter and sugar together until soft and light. Mash the chestnut purée down in a separate bowl until smooth and then add to the creamed mixture. Cool the chocolate slightly and then beat into the chestnut mixture. Turn into the loaf tin, level the top, and chill in the refrigerator until firm.

This pudding is best served very cold, so turn out onto a serving dish, cover with the whipped cream and leave in the refrigerator until required. Just before serving sprinkle with grated chocolate.

Serves 8 to 10

Nutty Brandy Snaps

Brandy snaps are tricky to make and take time, so for this recipe buy them. Usually they come in packets of 12, but remember they are brittle so treat with care and store in a tin.

Preparation time about 5 to 8 minutes

¼ pint (150 ml) double cream
a little icing sugar
1 oz (25 g) walnuts, finely chopped
2 teaspoons brandy
8 brandy snaps

Whisk the cream until it forms soft peaks and will hold its shape. Fold in the icing sugar to sweeten to taste, followed by the nuts and brandy, and mix well.

Pipe or spoon the cream mixture into the brandy snaps. Put on a plate and leave in the refrigerator for about an hour before serving.

Serves 4

Pears Orient Express

Very simple and special. Top with slices of kiwi fruit or sliced strawberries.

Preparation time about 10 minutes

15-oz (425-g) can pears, drained
2 oz (50 g) caster sugar
grated rind and juice of half a lemon
6 tablespoons white wine
½ pint (300 ml) double cream

Lightly mash the pears with a fork and divide between 4 glasses.

Place the sugar, lemon rind and juice and wine in a bowl and stir until the sugar has dissolved. Add the cream and whisk lightly until thick and then spoon on top of the pears.

Chill until required, then serve with shortbread fingers (see page 188).

Serves 4

Cherry Cream

Serve cold on the same day as it is made.

Preparation time about 5 minutes

½ pint (300 ml) double cream
½ pint (300 ml) natural yogurt
14-oz (397-g) can pitted black cherries
caster sugar

Whisk the cream until thick and then stir in the yogurt. Drain the cherries very well and fold into the mixture.

Turn into a small glass serving dish or individual dishes. Dust with caster sugar and chill in the refrigerator until required.

Serves 4

Strawberry Syllabub

An impressive yet simple ending for a dinner party.

Preparation time about 10 minutes

12 large strawberries
juice of 1 lemon
2 tablespoons sweet sherry
2 tablespoons brandy
2 oz (50 g) caster sugar
½ pint (300 ml) double cream

Line the insides of 4 stemmed glasses with slices of strawberries –
about 3 strawberries to each glass – and press the slices firmly onto the
glasses, making sure that they fit right into the bases.

Now prepare the syllabub. Put the lemon juice into a bowl with the
sherry, brandy and sugar and stir well until the sugar has dissolved.
Pour in the cream and whisk the mixture using an electric or hand
rotary whisk until it forms soft peaks.

Spoon the syllabub into the glasses and chill for at least an hour before
serving.

Serves 4

Whisky Flummery

Should you have egg yolks left over in the refrigerator this is an ideal way of using them up. It's best served cold, but can be served warm. If you've no whisky in the house, then use sherry or fresh lemon juice.

Preparation time about 10 minutes

4 egg yolks
3 tablespoons caster sugar
3 tablespoons whisky
½ pint (300 ml) double cream

Place the egg yolks and sugar in a bowl over a pan of boiling water and whisk until thick and creamy. Add the whisky and continue whisking until thick again. Cool.

Whisk the cream until thick and will hold a soft peak, and fold into the egg mixture. Spoon into glasses and then chill until required. Serve with thin crisp biscuits.

Serves 4

Scotch Mist

Guests will probably think you've spent hours preparing this, but in fact it only takes minutes. Gold almonds are quite expensive, but sugared almonds are a good substitute.

Preparation time about 8 minutes

½ pint (300 ml) double cream
3 tablespoons whisky
2 oz (50 g) meringues (see page 184)
Gold or sugared almonds to decorate

Whisk the cream and whisky together lightly until the mixture holds its shape. Place the meringues in a plastic bag and lightly crush, then fold into the cream and divide the mixture between 4 glasses.

Chill for about an hour before serving decorated with almonds.

Serves 4

Ice Cream Specials

Make these sundaes and parfaits up for however many portions you require. If you have the ingredients ready each will only take 3 to 4 minutes to assemble.

Peppermint Park Special

In the base of a tall glass put a few slices of canned peach, and top with a scoop of vanilla ice cream. Add a spoonful of chocolate toffee sauce (see page 153), repeat with a scoop of ice cream and then another spoonful of sauce. Finally add a dollop of thick cream and sprinkle with chopped nuts. Serve with a long spoon.

Coffee Yum Yum

Take a shallow dish and place 2 scoops of coffee and brandy ice cream (see page 157) side by side. Melt a Mars bar in a bowl over a pan of simmering water and then spoon a little over the ice cream. Put a swirl of cream on top and serve immediately with wafer biscuits.

Minted Moments

In the base of a tall glass place a scoop of mint chocolate chip ice cream. Cover with broken macaroons (see page 189), then add another scoop of ice cream. Trickle over a little Crème de Menthe, add a swirl of whipped cream and top with a chocolate mint. Serve with a long spoon.

Banana Suprême

Slice a small banana into the base of a shallow dish. Cover with scoops of chocolate ice cream (see page 157). Put a swirl of cream on each scoop and sprinkle with pistachio nuts. Serve with a fan wafer.

Tutti Fruiti Sundae

Take a sundae glass and fill with small scoops of tutti fruiti ice cream (see page 156). Spoon over candied chopped fruits that have been soaked in brandy, and top with a swirl of cream.

FAMILY FAVOURITES

I am sure that most families have their favourite puddings. These are all popular with us, sure to be greeted with exclamations of approval no matter how often they may appear. I have been serving them for years. Some have been handed on to me by my mother, others the children have discovered for themselves. Among the latter, my son Thomas's lemon flan has appeared in my books before, but I daren't leave it out. A mixture of condensed milk and lemon juice set in a digestive crust, it appeals to all age groups. So much so that by popular demand we had it recently at a family wedding reception!

Thomas's Lemon Flan

I make no apology for including this recipe again. It has appeared in most of my books and in my television programmes. It is Thomas's party piece and he makes it when we have a crowd for lunch. Decorate it with whatever you have to hand – try strawberries in season, halved grapes, chocolate buttons, Maltesers, whipped cream or anything from the store cupboard.

Preparation time about 10 minutes

> *4 oz (100 g) digestive biscuits*
> *2 oz (50 g) butter*
> *1 oz (25 g) demerara sugar*
> *½ pint (300 ml) double cream*
> *large can of condensed milk*
> *grated rind and juice of 2 large lemons*
> *a few grapes to decorate*

Put the biscuits in a polythene bag and crush with a rolling pin. Melt the butter in a small pan, add the sugar and stir in the biscuit crumbs and mix well. Turn into an 8- to 9-inch (20- to 22.5-cm) flan dish and press into shape around the base and sides with the back of a spoon.

Put the cream, condensed milk, lemon rind and juice in a bowl and whisk the mixture together until well blended. Pour into the flan case and leave to set. Decorate with halved grapes.

Serves 6 to 8

ɔn Fluff Pie

ringue pie with a delicious soft sharp centre.

) minutes
ınutes

nbs (see page 179)
ld water

f 2 lemons
6 oz (1/5 g) caster sugar

Heat the oven to 425°F, 220°C, gas mark 7. Put the pastry crumbs in a bowl, add the water and mix to a firm dough. Roll out on a floured surface and use to line an 8-inch (20-cm) flan tin. Line the flan with greaseproof paper and baking beans and bake blind for 10 minutes, then remove the baking beans and greaseproof paper and return to the oven and leave to dry out for a further 5 minutes.

Meanwhile make the filling. Place the egg yolks in a bowl with the lemon rind and juice and 4 oz (100 g) of the caster sugar. Stand over a pan of hot simmering water, and stir until the mixture is thick and will leave a trail (about 10 minutes).

Whisk the egg whites until stiff and then whisk in the remaining sugar a teaspoonful at a time. Remove the egg yolk bowl from the heat and stir in half the egg whites using a metal spoon. Turn into the flan and then cover with the remaining egg whites.

Turn the oven down to 300°F, 150°C, gas mark 3 and bake in the oven for 30 minutes until a pale golden brown. Serve either warm or cold. I find this a very good-natured dish and it will happily sit on the bottom of the oven under a casserole or cake to dry out the meringue.

Serves 6

Lemon Meringue Pie

Although this is quite difficult to get out of the dish for serving, it is really delicious and very lemony. If you don't want to make a biscuit base use a large sponge flan instead.

Preparation time about 20 minutes
Cooking time about 30 minutes

Crumb crust
  6 oz (175 g) digestive biscuits
  3 oz (75 g) butter
  1½ oz (40 g) demerara sugar

Filling
  2 large lemons
  1½ oz (40 g) cornflour
  ½ pint (300 ml) water
  2 egg yolks
  3 oz (75 g) caster sugar

Meringue topping
  3 egg whites
  4½ oz (125 g) caster sugar

First make the crumb crust. Put the biscuits in a polythene bag and crush with a rolling pin. Melt the butter in a small pan, add the sugar and stir in the crumbs and mix well. Turn into a 9-inch (22.5-cm) flan dish and press into shape around the base and sides with the back of a spoon.

For the fillings, grate the rind and squeeze the juice from the lemons and put in a bowl with the cornflour. Add 2 tablespoons of the water and blend to form a smooth paste. Boil the remaining water and pour onto the cornflour mixture. Return the cornflour to the pan, bring to the boil and simmer for 3 minutes until thick, stirring continually. Remove from the heat, add the egg yolks and sugar, then return to the heat for a minute to thicken the sauce. Cool slightly, then spoon the lemon filling into the flan.

Heat the oven to 325°F, 160°C, gas mark 3.

Whisk the egg whites with an electric or rotary whisk until they form stiff peaks, add the sugar a teaspoonful at a time, whisking well after each addition. Spoon over the lemon filling being careful to spread it right up to the edge of the pastry, leaving no air spaces. Place the pie in the oven for about 30 minutes or until the meringue is a pale golden brown.

Serve either warm or cold.

Serves 6 to 8

Lemon Cream Cheese

You could serve this mixture in a biscuit crust. (See page 78.)

Preparation time about 10 minutes

6 oz (175 g) cream cheese
2 oz (50 g) caster sugar
grated rind of 1 lemon
juice of half a lemon
2 eggs, separated
¼ pint (150 ml) double cream
lemon slices to decorate

Put the cream cheese and sugar in a bowl and cream together until smooth and soft. Add the lemon rind and juice with the egg yolks and blend thoroughly. Whisk the egg whites until stiff and whisk the cream until it forms soft peaks. Fold first the cream and then the egg whites through the lemon mixture.

Divide between 4 glasses or individual serving dishes and leave in a cool place until required. Decorate with lemon slices before serving, and if liked serve with shortbread fingers.

Serves 4

Lemon Soufflé Omelette

One of the fastest of puddings and must be eaten straight from the pan. Best made when there are only 2 for a meal, as doing large numbers slows down the proceedings.

Preparation time about 5 minutes
Cooking time about 5 to 7 minutes

2 large eggs
grated rind and juice of half a lemon
2 teaspoons caster sugar
½ oz (12.5 g) butter
lemon wedges

Separate the eggs and place the yolks in a basin with the lemon rind, juice and sugar. Beat well until pale and creamy. Whisk the egg whites, using a rotary or electric whisk, until they are just stiff. Mix 1 tablespoonful into the yolks and then carefully fold in the remainder.

Heat the omelette pan and then melt the butter in it over a moderate heat. Spread the mixture into the pan and cook without moving for 3 to 4 minutes until a pale golden brown underneath.

Slip the pan under a medium grill for 2 to 3 minutes to set the top. Make a slight cut across the centre of the omelette; fold in half and slide onto a warm serving dish. Sprinkle with a little caster sugar and serve with lemon wedges. Divide in half.

Serves 2

Jam Omelette

Omit the lemon rind and juice from the basic recipe and add 2 teaspoons cold water to the egg yolks. Make and cook as above, then spread one half with a rounded tablespoon of warmed jam (strawberry and black cherry are nice). Fold in half, slip onto a dish and sprinkle with icing sugar.

Golden Apple and Lemon Pudding

Golden granulated sugar – a natural unrefined sugar – is especially good for crumbles and topping, as it gives a golden colour. This pudding is rather like Eves pudding with a sponge on top of apple.

Preparation time about 15 minutes
Cooking time about 35 minutes

1¼ lb (550 g) cooking apples
4 oz (100 g) golden granulated sugar
juice and grated rind of 1 lemon
4 oz (100 g) self-raising flour
3 oz (75 g) soft margarine
1 egg
¼ pint (150 ml) milk

Heat the oven to 375°F, 190°C, gas mark 5, and lightly butter a 1½-pint (900-ml) pie dish.

Peel, core and slice the apples into a saucepan, add 2 oz (50 g) of the sugar and the lemon juice. Cover and cook slowly until the apple is soft, then turn into the pie dish.

Put the flour and margarine into a bowl and rub together until the mixture resembles fine breadcrumbs. Add the remaining sugar, the lemon rind, egg and milk and beat well to a pouring consistency and spoon over the apples.

Bake in the oven for about 35 minutes until risen and golden brown. Serve hot with custard.

Serves 4

Simple Apple Charlotte

Keep fresh white breadcrumbs in the freezer, then they are always ready for pudding, for stuffings, or bread sauce.

Preparation time about 10 minutes
Cooking time about 45 minutes

2 lb (900 g) cooking apples
4 tablespoons demerara sugar
6 oz (175 g) shredded suet
6 oz (175 g) fresh white breadcrumbs

Heat the oven to 375°F, 190°C, gas mark 5.

Peel, core and slice the apples thinly. Mix the sugar, suet and breadcrumbs together.

Place a layer of apples in the base of a greased ovenproof dish, then add a layer of dry ingredients, then a layer of apples. Alternate until all the apples are used, finishing with a layer of dry ingredients.

Bake in the oven for about 45 minutes or until the top is crisp and golden brown and the apple tender. Serve hot with custard.

Serves 6

Sliced Apple Suet Puddings

When the Christmas holidays are coming to an end or the weather is cold, these are highly appreciated.

Preparation time about 5 minutes
Cooking time about 1 hour

a good pinch cinnamon
2 oz (50 g) demerara sugar
4 oz (100 g) peeled cooking apple, diced
4 oz (100 g) self-raising flour
2 oz (50 g) shredded suet
about 5 tablespoons cold water

Stir the cinnamon into the demerara sugar and roll the apple pieces in the sugar so that they are well coated.

Mix the flour with the suet and then stir in the apple and sugar mixture. Add just sufficient water to mix to a light but not sticky dough. Turn into 4 old, well greased, handle-less cups (or use a 1-pint or 600-ml pudding basin). Cover with pieces of greased greaseproof paper with a pleat in the centre and lids of doubled foil. Put in a saucepan with boiling water to come halfway up the sides of the cups. Cover the saucepan with a tight fitting lid and boil gently for about 1 hour, topping up with more boiling water if necessary. (A larger basin would take about 1½ to 2 hours to cook.)

Remove the foil and greaseproof paper and turn out onto warm plates. Serve with golden syrup.

Serves 4

Pineapple Pudding

All made from ingredients that you are likely to have on the larder shelf, this pudding should be served warm.

Preparation time about 10 to 12 minutes
Cooking time about 30 minutes

15-oz (427-g) can pineapple pieces
about ½ pint (300 ml) milk
2 oz (50 g) butter
2 oz (50 g) flour
4½ oz (125 g) caster sugar
2 eggs, separated

Heat the oven to 325°F, 160°C, gas mark 3. Drain the syrup from the pineapple into a measure and then make up to ¾ pint (450 ml) with milk.

Melt the butter in a saucepan, stir in the flour and cook for a minute. Add the milk mixture and bring to the boil, stirring, until the sauce has thickened. Cook for 2 minutes and then stir in 1½ oz (40 g) of the caster sugar until dissolved. Remove from the heat and beat in the egg yolks. Stir in the pineapple pieces and turn the mixture into a 2½-pint (1.4-litre) ovenproof dish.

Whisk the egg whites with an electric or hand rotary whisk until stiff and then whisk in the remaining sugar a teaspoonful at a time. Pile the meringue on top of the pineapple mixture, making sure that it comes right to the edge of the dish. Bake in the oven for about 30 minutes until the meringue is a pale golden brown and crisp.

Serves 4 to 6

Plum Fool

I made this with plums because they give an attractive pink appearance to the fool, but try ringing the changes by using greengages or cherries.

Preparation time about 10 minutes

> *1 lb, 4-oz (567-g) can Victoria plums*
> *¼ pint (150 ml) natural yogurt*
> *a little caster sugar*
> *¼ pint (150 ml) double cream*

Drain the syrup from the plums and keep on one side and use next time you are making a jelly or trifle. Remove any stones from the fruit, place flesh in a blender and purée until smooth. Blend in the yogurt for about 30 seconds then taste the mixture and add a little caster sugar to taste.

Place the double cream in a bowl and lightly whisk until it forms soft peaks. Stir in the plum purée until evenly blended and then turn into a glass dish and leave in a cool place until required.

I like to serve this with shortbread fingers (see page 188).

Serves 4

Apricot Creams

Apricots and chocolate are a delicious combination and this is always a great favourite with my family. (*See picture facing page 128.*)

Preparation time about 20 minutes

1 egg white
2 oz (50 g) caster sugar
1/4 pint (150 ml) whipping cream
2 tablespoons brandy
1 oz (25 g) flaked almonds
5 chocolate flake bars
14 1/2-oz (411-g) can apricot halves

Whisk the egg white until stiff and then whisk in the caster sugar a teaspoonful at a time. Whisk the cream until thick and then whisk in the brandy. Fold in the egg white, with half the flaked almonds and two of the crumbled chocolate flakes.

Purée the apricots in a blender or processor with a spoonful of the juice. Brown the remaining almonds under the grill, then cool.

Spoon a little of the apricot purée into the bottom of 6 individual glasses, then cover with a layer of cream and then repeat with another layer of apricot purée and a final layer of cream. Sprinkle with the toasted almonds and then stick half a chocolate flake into each just before serving.

Serves 6

Blackberry and Apple Trifle

Trifle is popular, but this one makes a change from the usual.

Preparation time about 30 minutes

> *8 trifle sponge cakes*
> *bramble jam*
> *2 macaroons (see page 189)*
> *¼ pint (150 ml) sweet white wine*
> *1 large cooking apple*
> *8 oz (225 g) blackberries*
> *1 tablespoon granulated sugar*

Custard
> *3 egg yolks*
> *1 oz (25 g) caster sugar*
> *2 teaspoons cornflour*
> *½ pint (300 ml) milk*
> *¼ pint (150 ml) whipping cream*
> *1 oz (25 g) toasted flaked almonds to decorate*

Split the sponge cakes, spread with bramble jam and sandwich together again. Cut each sponge into 6 pieces and place in the base of a 9-inch (22.5-cm) shallow glass dish. Crumble the macaroons on top and then moisten with the wine.

Peel, core and slice the apple, place in a small saucepan with the blackberries and sugar, and simmer for 5 minutes until the sugar has dissolved and the juices have run. Cool and spread over sponges.

To make the custard, place the egg yolks, sugar and cornflour in a bowl and mix well. Place the milk in a small saucepan and heat gently until hand hot. Pour onto the egg yolks, stirring constantly, then return to the pan and cook gently over a low heat, stirring until the mixture thickens. Do not boil or it will curdle. Cool and pour over the fruit and leave to set. Whisk the cream until it forms soft peaks and then spread over the trifle and sprinkle with almonds.

Serves 6 to 8

Hot Swiss Trifle

This is best made in an ovenproof glass dish so that the slices of Swiss roll show through.

Preparation time about 15 minutes
Cooking time about 20 minutes

1 Swiss roll
14½-oz (411-g) can apricots, drained
2 tablespoons custard powder
2 eggs, separated
1 tablespoon granulated sugar
1 pint (600 ml) milk
4 oz (100 g) caster sugar
1 oz (25 g) blanched halved almonds

Heat the oven to 350°F, 180°C, gas mark 4. Slice the Swiss roll and arrange with the apricots in a 2-pint (1-litre) ovenproof dish.

Blend the custard powder, egg yolks and granulated sugar with a little of the milk. Heat the remaining milk and when nearly boiling, stir onto the mixed custard powder. Return to the saucepan and bring to the boil, stirring continuously and when thick, pour over the apricots.

Whisk the egg whites until stiff and then whisk in the caster sugar a teaspoonful at a time. Pile or pipe the meringue on top of the custard and then stud with the almonds. Bake in the oven for 20 minutes until the meringue is tinged golden brown.

Serves 4

Boozy Orange Pancakes

Make a batch of basic pancakes and try one of the easy recipes on the next few pages; let one member of the family make the pancakes and the other be in charge of the filling.

Preparation time 10 minutes
Cooking time about 15 to 20 minutes

2 oranges
1 lemon
4 oz (100 g) unsalted butter
2 oz (50 g) icing sugar, sieved
2 tablespoons sweet sherry
8 pancakes (see page 186)
2 oz (50 g) granulated sugar

Heat the oven to 375°F, 190°C, gas mark 5. Grate the rind finely off 1 orange and half the lemon, then squeeze the juices of all the fruit.

Beat the butter, sugar and orange and lemon rind together until well blended and then beat in 1 tablespoon of sherry. Spread this mixture over the pancakes and then fold each pancake in quarters and arrange overlapping in a shallow ovenproof dish.

Place the orange and lemon juice in a saucepan with the sugar and bring to the boil, so that the sugar dissolves. Boil rapidly for 3 minutes, then remove from the heat, cool slightly, and add the remaining sherry. Pour over the pancakes, cover with foil and place in the oven for about 15 to 20 minutes until hot.

Serves 4

Honey and Banana Pancakes

These can be decorated with more slices of banana. (*See picture facing page 65.*)

8 pancakes (see page 186)
5 tablespoons clear honey
juice of 1 lemon
pinch of mixed spice
4 medium-sized bananas
a few toasted flaked almonds

Heat the pancakes in the oven at 375°F, 190°C, gas mark 5, wrapped in foil, for about 20 minutes.

Heat together the honey, lemon juice and spice. Thinly slice the bananas, add to the pan and mix gently into the honey mixture.

Divide the mixture between the pancakes and fold each pancake into four. Sprinkle with almonds and serve at once.

Serves 4

Pancake Meringue

A very good way to use up the odd egg white.

8 pancakes (see page 186)
1 egg white
2 oz (50 g) caster sugar
jam or lemon curd
a few flaked almonds

Heat the pancakes in the oven at 375°F, 190°C, gas mark 5, wrapped in foil, for about 20 minutes. Then turn the oven up to 450°F, 230°C, gas mark 8.

Whisk the egg white until stiff and then whisk in the caster sugar a teaspoonful at a time until all has been added.

Sandwich the pancakes together on an ovenproof serving dish with the jam or lemon curd. Pipe or swirl the meringue over the top of the pancakes and sprinkle with flaked almonds. Bake in the oven for about 2 to 3 minutes until the meringue is lightly brown. Serve at once cut in wedges as for a cake.

Serves 4

Caramel Tart

This is a top favourite with my family. Condensed milk makes a marvellous creamy caramel when boiled gently, still in the can, then cooled. If I know I am going to make this tart I stand a can in an old cake tin half full of water when I am using the oven on a Sunday morning. Then I leave it to cool, and put it, unopened, in the refrigerator until I need it.

Preparation time about 10 minutes
Cooking time about 3½ hours

> *14-oz (397-g) can condensed milk*
> *4 oz (100 g) digestive biscuits*
> *2 oz (50 g) butter*
> *1 oz (25 g) demerara sugar*
> *2 oz (50 g) chopped walnuts*

Bring a small saucepan of water to the boil with an unopened can of condensed milk in it, then cover and cook gently for about 3½ hours, checking from time to time to see that the can is still covered with water. Remove and leave to cool before opening.

To make the biscuit base, crush the biscuits in a polythene bag. Melt the butter in a saucepan and add the sugar and biscuits and mix well. Spoon into an 8-inch (20-cm) loose bottomed flan tin and press firmly over the base and sides, using the back of a metal spoon. Chill.

Open the can of condensed milk, put in a bowl and beat well. It will be a caramel colour and will have thickened. Spread into the biscuit crust, and sprinkle with chopped walnuts. Leave in the refrigerator until required.

Serves 6

Crème à la Framboise

This is also good made with bramble jelly.

Preparation time about 12 to 15 minutes

  3 large eggs, separated
  6 oz (175 g) seedless raspberry jam
  1 tablespoon lemon juice

Put the egg yolks into a bowl over a pan of simmering water. Add the raspberry jam and whisk the mixture over the heat until it has thickened (when the whisk is lifted out it will leave a trail). This will take about 5 to 7 minutes. Take the mixture from the pan and whisk for 2 to 3 minutes to cool.

Whisk the egg whites with a rotary or electric hand whisk until stiff and then fold into the raspberry mixture with the lemon juice.

Pour into 4 large or 6 small individual glass serving dishes and leave in the refrigerator to chill until required.

Serves 4 to 6

Byre Farm
Christmas Pudding

A rich dark special Christmas pudding, the best I have tasted, which has been in my sister-in-law's family for years. It's really speedy on Christmas Day as it only needs just one hour's boiling (or simmering, as all the boiling is done ahead).

Preparation time about 10 minutes
Cooking time 8 hours boiling in advance and 1 hour on Christmas Day

6 oz (175 g) raisins
3 oz (75 g) each of currants and sultanas
2 oz (50 g) each of candied peel and nuts, chopped
3 oz (75 g) self-raising flour
2 eggs
4 oz (100 g) fresh white breadcrumbs
4 oz (100 g) shredded suet
1/2 pint (300 ml) stout
1 cooking apple, peeled, cored and diced
grated rind and juice of 1 orange and 1 lemon
2 tablespoons black treacle
1/2 teaspoon each of nutmeg and mixed spice

Grease a 2-pint (a good litre) pudding basin.

Place all the ingredients together in a large bowl and mix together very thoroughly. Turn into the basin, cover the top with greased greaseproof paper and a foil lid. Simmer in a pan of boiling water for 8 hours.

Remove from the pan, cool, cover with a fresh piece of foil and store until Christmas Day. Then simmer for 1 hour, turn out and serve hot with the usual accompaniments.

Serves 10 to 12

FRUIT IN SEASON
AND OUT

Fruit is versatile, quick and easy to prepare, and a universal favourite. Take strawberries or raspberries. At the height of their all too short summer season we can't get too many of them, just as they are, heaped in a bowl and eaten with sugar and thick cream. Later they can be used more sparingly, in strawberry or raspberry shortcake, in fools or mouses, in purées and as flavouring for fruit sauces.

A perfect peach, ripe and glowing, or a well polished rosy apple can in themselves be the ideal finish to a meal and need no preparation. But peaches, apples, pears, cherries, plums, fruit of all kinds, are the basis of innumerable puddings, hot or cold, light or substantial. There are fruit tarts, crumbles, baked apples, fruit salads of different kinds, trifle, mousses. Serve fresh fruit in season when it is at its least expensive and while it is plentiful take the chance to stock up your freezer for the months to come.

Try unusual mixtures. Most people know how good strawberries are with a little fresh orange juice as a change from cream. But try raspberries with melon, or make a raspberry and apple crumble.

Chilled whole fruits like melon or grapes are simplicity itself and should please your guests. Fresh fruit is the basis of fruit salad but you can give it variety with the addition of canned. Fruit salad, by the way, should always be served well chilled. Give a festive touch to stewed fruit with a meringue topping which is quick and easy to make. Cream is the natural accompaniment to most fruit puddings, but for economy's sake you can always use custard, or even yogurt.

Strawberry Shortcake

With this shortcake you can make a few strawberries go a long way!

Preparation time about 15 minutes
Cooking time about 15 minutes

Shortcake
   4 oz (100 g) flour
   1½ oz (40 g) caster sugar
   3 oz (75 g) butter
   1 egg yolk

Topping
   1 lb (450 g) strawberries
   4 tablespoons redcurrant jelly
   1 tablespoon water

Heat the oven to 375°F, 190°C, gas mark 7.

Put the flour and sugar into a bowl and make a well in the centre. Put the butter, cut in small pieces, and the egg yolk into the well and gradually work all the ingredients together with the fingertips. Pat the shortcake mixture into a round on a baking sheet about 8 inches (20 cm) in diameter. Bake in the oven for about 15 minutes until a pale golden brown, remove and leave to cool

Place the shortcake on a serving dish and arrange the strawberries cut in half, on top. Put the redcurrant jelly in a small saucepan with the water and heat gently until melted. Brush all over the strawberries. Serve with a bowl of lightly whipped cream.

Serves 6 to 8

Strawberry Cream Gâteau

A very good way to serve the first strawberries of the season, it is also perfect with raspberries.

Preparation time about 10 minutes

2 × 7 inch (17.5 cm) sponge cakes (see page 180)
½ pint (300 ml) double cream
8 oz (225 g) strawberries
a little caster sugar

Place 1 cake on a serving dish. Whisk the cream until thick and place two-thirds in a small bowl. Leave 6 whole strawberries on one side for decoration and then roughly chop the remainder and stir into the larger quantity of cream, adding a little sugar to taste. Pile this cream mixture onto the sponge cake making a slight dome in the centre.

Cut the remaining sponge into 6 even wedges and then arrange on the top of the cake. The domed surface will cause the points to stand up in the centre, showing the strawberry filling. The outside of the cake is held in place by the cream.

Using the remaining cream pipe a rosette on each portion of sponge and then decorate with the whole strawberries.

Serves 6

Raspberry and Melon Salad

Out of season use frozen raspberries and then there will be no need to chill the salad as the thawing raspberries will do this.

Preparation time about 10 minutes

1 lb (450 g) fresh raspberries
2 to 4 oz (50 to 100 g) caster sugar
2 to 3 tablespoons Grand Marnier or Kirsch
1 ripe melon

Put the raspberries into a bowl and sprinkle with sugar and liqueur and leave in a cool place for at least an hour to become juicy.

Peel the melon, remove the seeds and cut into small cubes. Stir into the raspberries and chill well.

Turn into a glass dish before serving with thin cream.

Serves 8

Chilled Citrus Fruit, Melon and Grapes

Very refreshing, goes well after a rich main course such as pork or meat in a creamy sauce.

Preparation time about 15 minutes

8 oz (225 g) black grapes, seeded
juice of a satsuma or tangerine
1 honeydew melon, cubed
1 grapefruit, segmented
2 oz (50 g) caster sugar

Place all the ingredients in a bowl and mix thoroughly. Cover with a piece of cling film and chill in the refrigerator before serving.

When required divide the mixture between 6 glasses to serve. You will find that it is not necessary to serve cream with this.

Serves 6

Exotic Fruit Salad

A delicious combination of fruit, serve this for a special meal. (*See picture facing page 129.*)

Preparation time about 10 minutes

1 large pineapple
3 oz (75 g) dates, stoned and halved
3 oz (75 g) strawberries, halved
2 kiwi fruit, peeled and sliced
a few black grapes, halved and seeded
1 to 2 tablespoons Kirsch

Cut the pineapple in half lengthways and scoop out the flesh to leave 2 thin shells.

Cut the pineapple flesh into neat pieces, trimming away the hard centre core. Place in a bowl, add all the other fruits and mix together lightly. Sprinkle over the Kirsch, pile the mixture back into the shells, cover with cling film and chill in the refrigerator for 1 to 2 hours before serving. Or you can chill the fruit in the bowl and turn into the pineapple shells just before serving. You can also add a little caster sugar if liked when mixing before chilling.

Serves 6

Pineapple and Grape Salad

A fresh tasting pudding, to be prepared when pineapples are at their best and cheapest.

Preparation time about 10 to 12 minutes

1 large pineapple
8 oz (225 g) white seedless grapes
2 level tablespoons caster sugar
2 tablespoons Kirsch or brandy
2 tablespoons lemon juice

Cut away the top and bottom of the pineapple and then cut across into four slices. Scoop out almost all the flesh from the slices, leaving enough to form a case with a base. Stand each case on a serving plate. Cut the pineapple flesh into small pieces, remove the core and discard. Place the flesh into a bowl with the remaining ingredients and mix well. Cover with a piece of fling film and leave in the refrigerator until required.

When ready to serve, divide the fruit between the pineapple cases and serve with a bowl of cream.

Serves 4

Pineapple Mousse

A light refreshing pudding that is ideal to serve after a heavy meal. Sometimes I make it in small plastic pots and take on a picnic.

Preparation time about 15 to 20 minutes

4 eggs
4 oz (100 g) caster sugar
1 large lemon
½ oz (12.5 g) gelatine
13¼-oz (376-g) can crushed pineapple

Separate the eggs, place the yolks in a bowl with the sugar and beat well until blended and creamy. Put the whites in another bowl ready for whisking. Grate the rind and squeeze the juice from the lemon and add to the yolk mixture.

Place the gelatine in a small bowl and add the drained juice from the pineapple, leave for 3 minutes until thick, then stand the bowl in a pan of simmering water and allow the gelatine to dissolve. Cool slightly and then add to the egg yolk mixture. Leave to cool but not set.

Whisk the egg whites, using a rotary or electric whisk until stiff, then fold into the egg yolks with the crushed pineapple.

Turn the mixture into a glass serving dish about 2 pints (a good litre) in size. Chill in the refrigerator for about 2 hours to set.

Serves 6 to 8

Chilled Mango Syllabub

This should be made on the day it is required as it tends to separate if kept.

Preparation time about 10 minutes

1 large ripe mango
1 glass white wine
juice of 1 small lemon
3 egg whites
4 oz (100 g) caster sugar
½ pint (300 ml) double cream

Peel the mango and cut the flesh from the stone, then reduce to a purée in a blender or food processor with the wine and lemon juice.

Whisk the egg whites until stiff and then gradually whisk in the sugar a teaspoonful at a time. Whisk the cream until it forms soft peaks, then fold into the purée. Fold in the egg whites.

Pour into a serving dish and leave in a cool place until required.

Serves 4

Bergen Lemon Cream

I first made this when I was Cookery Editor of *Ideal Home* magazine, and I still get letters from people who continue to make it. It's very simple, and if time is short leave out the whipped egg whites and use whipping cream instead. A good way of using up broken meringues.

Preparation time about 5 to 8 minutes

½ pint (300 ml) double cream
finely grated rind and juice of 3 lemons
2 oz (50 g) caster sugar
2 egg whites
3 large broken meringues (see page 184)

Put the cream, lemon rind and juice with the sugar in a bowl and whisk the mixture until it forms soft peaks.

In another bowl whisk the egg whites until they form stiff peaks, then fold into the cream mixture with the broken pieces of meringues.

Turn into 6 individual dishes and then leave in the refrigerator until required.

Serves 6

Key Lemon Pie

This is a recipe that originally came from Key West in Florida where they make it with limes.

Preparation time about 15 minutes
Cooking time about 25 minutes

Biscuit case
   5 oz (150 g) digestive biscuits
   2½ oz (65 g) butter
   1 oz (25 g) sugar

Filling
   2 eggs, separated
   7-oz (200-g) can condensed milk
   grated rind and juice of 1 lemon

Heat the oven to 350°F, 180°C, gas mark 4. Place a 9-inch (22.5-cm) loose-bottomed flan tin on a baking tray.

Put the biscuits in a plastic bag and roll with a rolling pin until fine crumbs. Melt the butter in a small saucepan, then add the biscuit crumbs and sugar and mix thoroughly. Place in the flan tin, pressing down well over the base and up the sides to form a case.

For the filling, place the egg yolks and condensed milk in a bowl and mix together, then stir in the lemon rind and juice until the mixture thickens. Whisk the egg whites until stiff and then fold through the lemon mixture. Turn into the flan case and smooth the top.

Bake in the oven for about 20 to 25 minutes, until set and starting to turn golden brown at the edges. Serve warm or cold.

Serves 6

Orange Compote

Fresh oranges are refreshing after a rich meal. Serve in small glasses or bowls, well chilled, and there is no need for cream.

Preparation time about 15 minutes

8 thin skinned oranges
2 oz (50 g) caster sugar
2 tablespoons orange liqueur

Using a sharp knife cut the peel from the oranges in a spiral so that all the pith is removed, then cut the oranges across into thin slices.

Arrange the slices of orange so that they overlap, in a glass bowl, and sprinkle with sugar and liqueur.

Leave in a cool place until the sugar has dissolved.

Serves 8

Toffee Pears

One of our favourite fruity puddings.

Preparation time about 8 minutes
Cooking time about 25 minutes

4 pears
2 oz (50 g) butter
4 oz (100 g) demerara or light soft brown sugar

Heat the oven to 400°F, 200°C, gas mark 6.

Peel, halve and core the pears and lay flat side down in an ovenproof dish in a single layer. Dot with butter and then sprinkle over the sugar and bake in the oven for about 25 minutes or until the pears are tender.

Serve straight from the dish in which they were cooked, spooning a little of the sauce over each portion. Serve with a jug of single cream.

Serves 4

Glorious Pears

In season use poached fresh pears if time allows.

Preparation time about 10 minutes
Cooking time about 55 minutes

> 6 oz (175 g) pastry crumbs (see page 179), or use an 8-inch
>   (20-cm) pastry flan case
> about 1½ tablespoons cold water

Filling
> 15-oz (425-g) can pear halves
> ¼ pint (150 ml) double cream
> 2 oz (50 g) caster sugar
> 1 teaspoon vanilla essence

Heat the oven to 400°F, 200°C, gas mark 6.

Place the pastry crumbs in a bowl and add sufficient water to mix to a firm dough. Roll out thinly on a floured surface and line an 8-inch (20-cm) flan ring, which should be placed on a baking sheet. Prick the base with a fork. Fill with greaseproof paper and baking beans and bake in the oven for 10 minutes then remove the paper and beans and return to the oven and bake for a further 5 minutes to dry out. Remove the flan from the oven and turn the heat down to 375°F, 190°C, gas mark 5.

Drain the pears and arrange over the base of the flan. Blend the cream, sugar and vanilla essence together and pour over the pears. Return to the oven for about 40 minutes. Serve either hot or cold.

Serves 6

William Pears in Cream

Choose ripe pears and bake them whilst enjoying the main course.

Preparation time about 5 minutes
Cooking time about 25 minutes

4 pears
2 oz (50 g) butter
¼ pint (150 ml) double cream
a little light soft brown sugar

Heat the oven to 350°F, 180°C, gas mark 4.

Peel, core and neatly slice the pears. Heat the butter in a frying pan and fry the pears for about 10 minutes or until just tender, so that they do not brown. Turn into an ovenproof serving dish.

Pour over the cream and bake in the oven for about 15 minutes, when the cream will have slightly thickened. Remove from the oven and sprinkle with a little soft brown sugar and serve at once.

Serves 4

Peaches in Brandy

It is best to serve these peaches very cold, and they are perfect after a heavy dinner. (*Illustrated on the jacket.*)

Preparation time about 15 minutes

4 oz (100 g) granulated sugar
½ pint (300 ml) water
8 ripe peaches
3 to 4 tablespoons brandy

Put the sugar in a saucepan with the water and heat gently over a low heat until it has dissolved, then remove and leave to cool.

Put the peaches in a basin and cover with boiling water. Leave for a minute, then turn all the peaches at once into a bowl of cold water and remove the skins by gently peeling them off. Prick each peach with a stainless steel fork right through to the stone in several places. As each peach is peeled and pricked put them in a glass bowl just big enough to take them.

Pour over the sugar syrup and then add the brandy so that the peaches are completely covered. Cover with a piece of cling film and chill for about 5 to 6 hours before serving, with a bowl of thick whipped cream.

Serves 8

Fresh Apricots in Cider

These apricots are gently poached whole in syrup, cider and orange juice. Serve very cold with whipped cream.

Preparation time about 2 to 3 minutes
Cooking time about 20 minutes

1½ lb (675 g) fresh apricots
6 oz (175 g) granulated sugar
1 orange
sweet cider
about ¼ teaspoon cinnamon

Wash the apricots and place in a saucepan with the sugar. Remove the rind from the orange in long strips using a potato peeler and add to the pan. Squeeze the juice from the orange, place in a measure and make up to ½ pint (300 ml) with cider. Pour into the saucepan and then cook the apricots gently for about 15 minutes or until they are tender but still whole.

Lift out the apricots with a slotted spoon and put in a glass serving dish. Boil the syrup rapidly until reduced by about half and then spoon over the apricots. Leave to cool, then chill well before serving.

Serves 4 to 6

Apricot Meringue

If you want a faster pudding make it in ramekins.

Preparation time about 10 minutes
Cooking time abut 45 minutes

    1 lb, 13-oz (800-g) can apricots, drained
    3 tablespoons brandy, liqueur or lemon juice
    1 oz (25 g) caster sugar
    2 egg yolks

Meringue
    2 egg whites
    4 oz (100 g) caster sugar

Heat the oven to 275°F, 140°C, gas mark 1.

Purée the apricots in a blender or processor, then add the brandy, sugar and egg yolks and mix well. Turn into a 1½-pint (900-ml) straight sided ovenproof dish.

To prepare the meringue, whisk the egg whites with a rotary or electric hand whisk until stiff and then whisk in 2 oz (50 g) sugar a teaspoonful at a time. Fold in the remaining sugar all at once. Spoon the meringue over the apricot purée and swirl into peaks.

Bake in the oven for about 45 minutes until crisp and golden. Serve hot or cold.

Serves 6

Apricot Crunch

If time is really short use a can of apricot pie filling and half the amount of breadcrumbs and sugar.

Preparation time about 15 minutes
Cooking time about 20 minutes

1 lb (450 g) fresh apricots
5 oz (150 g) caster sugar
1 oz (25 g) butter
2 teacups fresh brown breadcrumbs
¼ pint (150 ml) double cream
a little grated chocolate

Place the apricots in a saucepan with a very little water and cook very slowly until soft (about 15 minutes). Remove from the heat, take out the stones and then mash to a purée and sweeten with about 3 oz (75 g) of the sugar.

Melt the butter in a baking tin, mix in the breadcrumbs and remaining caster sugar, and put in a hot oven at 400°F, 200°C, gas mark 6 for about 5 minutes or until golden brown and crisp. Remove and leave to cool.

Place a layer of the crumbs in a shallow 1¼-pint (750-ml) dish, put a layer of apricot purée on top, then repeat with layers of crumbs and apricot, finishing with apricot purée.

Whisk the double cream until it is just beginning to thicken and form soft peaks and spread all over the apricot. Sprinkle with grated chocolate and serve.

Serves 4

Plum and Almond Crumble

Plums and almonds are a good combination and this homely pudding makes the most of them. Serve hot from the oven with plenty of thin pouring cream.

Preparation time about 15 minutes
Cooking time about 40 minutes

4 oz (100 g) plain flour
2 oz (50 g) ground almonds
3 oz (75 g) margarine
2 oz (50 g) light soft brown sugar
1½ lb (675 g) plums
4 oz (100 g) caster sugar
1 oz (25 g) flaked almonds

Heat the oven to 400°F, 200°C, gas mark 6.

Place the flour in a bowl with the almonds, add the margarine cut in small pieces, and rub in with the fingertips until the mixture resembles fine breadcrumbs. Stir in the brown sugar.

Cut the plums in half, remove the stones and put in a pie dish with the caster sugar. Spoon over the crumble mixture and sprinkle with the flaked almonds. Bake in the oven for about 40 minutes or until the crumble and almonds are golden brown and the plums tender.

Serves 6

Raspberry and Apple Crumble

Make as above but use 12 oz (350 g) cooking apples, peeled, cored and sliced, and 12 oz (350 g) raspberries. This is a good way of using the last of the raspberries and the first of the windfall cooking apples.

Apple Snow

I have used apples in this recipe, but a great many different fruits can be used to make snows – try rhubarb, apricot, plum or gooseberries. Cook the fruit, then purée, and allow 1 lb (450 g) raw fruit to each 2 egg whites.

Preparation time about 20 minutes

1 lb (450 g) cooking apples
2 tablespoons water
a knob of butter
2 strips of lemon peel
2 to 3 oz (50 to 75 g) caster sugar
a little green colouring
2 egg whites

Peel and core the apples and then cut in slices. Place in a saucepan with the water, butter, and lemon peel. Cover the pan with a tight fitting lid and cook gently for about 15 minutes, stirring occasionally, until the apples are soft and fluffy.

Remove the pan from the heat, take out the strips of lemon and discard, then stir in sugar to taste. Purée the apples either by sieving or putting in the blender or processor. Add a few drops of green colouring, then leave to cool.

Whisk the egg whites until stiff with a rotary or electric hand whisk. Fold into the apple purée until evenly blended. Turn into a glass serving dish and chill until ready to serve. I find that this dish is best eaten quite quickly after making.

Serves 4

Hot Apple Scone

Serve with a big bowl of lightly whipped cream, or if liked, split and serve with butter. (*See picture facing page 160.*)

Preparation time about 15 minutes
Cooking time about 12 to 15 minutes

Scone dough
    8 oz (225 g) self-raising flour
    2 oz (50 g) butter
    2 oz (50 g) caster sugar
    about ¼ pint (150 ml) milk

Filling and topping
    12 oz (350 g) cooking apples, peeled, cored and sliced
    4 tablespoons apricot jam

Heat the oven to 425°F, 220°C, gas mark 7. Lightly grease a baking tray.

Place the flour in a bowl, add the butter cut in small pieces and rub in with the fingertips until the mixture resembles fine breadcrumbs. Add the sugar, then mix to a soft dough with the milk, and turn onto a lightly floured surface. Knead quickly and then divide into two equal sized pieces. Roll each piece into a circle about 7 inches (17.5 cm) in diameter. Lift one piece onto the greased baking tray. Arrange half the apple slices over the piece of scone dough and then cover with the remaining scone dough. Arrange the remaining apple slices on top.

Heat the apricot jam gently and brush over the top of the apple. Bake in the oven for 12 to 15 minutes until the scone is golden brown. Serve cut in wedges.

Serves 6

Apple and Lemon Tart

The filling sets like a custard, and is sharp, tasting like lemon curd. Very good served cold with a bowl of lightly whipped cream.

Preparation time about 15 minutes
Cooking time about 25 minutes

1×8-inch (20-cm) baked pastry flan case

Filling
4 eggs
6 oz (175 g) caster sugar
2 oz (50 g) butter
grated rind and juice of 2 lemons
1 cooking apple

Heat the oven to 350°F, 180°C, gas mark 4. Place the flan case on a baking sheet, or ovenproof plate.

Place the eggs, sugar and butter in a bowl and put over a pan of hot water until the butter has melted and the sugar dissolved, stirring continuously. Then add the lemon rind and juice.

Peel, core and slice the apple thinly in a single layer over the base of the flan case and sprinkle with a little extra caster sugar. Pour the filling over and then place in the oven and bake for about 25 minutes, when the filling will have set. Remove and leave to cool on the baking sheet until the tart is quite cold then transfer to a serving dish. If you bake the tart on an ovenproof plate, it will not be necessary to move it.

Serves 6

Kissel

This is a Danish recipe that can be made using either redcurrants or raspberries.

Preparation time about 10 to 12 minutes

2 level tablespoons cornflour
¼ level teaspoon ground cinnamon
1 rounded tablespoon granulated sugar
¼ pint (150 ml) water
1 orange
8 oz (225 g) redcurrants or raspberries
caster sugar

Place the cornflour, cinnamon and sugar in a saucepan, blend in the water and bring to the boil, stirring continuously until the mixture has thickened. Simmer for about 1 minute.

Grate the rind and squeeze the juice from the orange and add both to the saucepan.

Strip the redcurrants from their stalks and stir into the hot sauce, taste, and if liked add a little sugar (if using currants I find a little extra sugar is sometimes necessary although not usually for raspberries). Heat through for a minute and then divide the mixture between 4 small glasses and sprinkle over a little caster sugar to prevent a skin forming.

Leave to cool and serve with almond biscuits (see page 187).

Serves 4

CHOCOLATE WITH EVERYTHING

Chocolate is the flavour of the month – this month or any other – the top favourite with young and old. It goes into puddings hot and cold, soufflés, trifles, sponges, meringues. It makes sauce for ice cream, icing for cakes. Chocolate gâteau can be served for pudding or for tea. Celebration cake is a special treat for the big occasion and if there is any left over you can cut it into wedges and freeze it for another day.

Chocolate makes one of the quickest and most effective decorations for puddings. Plain chocolate is better than milk for grating or melting, but plain real chocolate is best of all. Grated chocolate can be sprinkled on trifles, gâteaux, mousses or ice cream. To melt it you do not need intense heat. It melts on a sunny windowsill, or in a child's pocket in summer. The easiest and least messy way is to break the chocolate into pieces and melt it slowly in a small bowl over a pan of hot water until it reaches pouring consistency.

To make chocolate curls the plain chocolate flavour cake covering works best. Simply spread melted 'chocolate' with a palette knife on a marble surface or laminated chopping board. Hold a cook's knife at an angle of rather less than 45 degrees to the board and slide it over the surface. The chocolate will make most satisfactory curls to decorate puddings or gâteaux. What you don't need at once you can store in the freezer.

Melted chocolate makes a banana dish beloved by children. Put pieces of chocolate in a *thick* polythene bag and let them melt slowly. Then simply snip a corner of the bag, squeeze the chocolate over the bananas and serve with cream. Or you can dip the bananas in melted chocolate and leave to set.

You don't even need to melt or grate chocolate for decoration. Use what you've got on hand – Maltesers can be very effective, or After Eights cut in half. Melted Mars bars make instant chocolate sauce (I try not to think about the calories!). For more special puddings, remember that brandy and rum go very well in chocolate recipes.

Midnight Mousse

This is a really dark frozen chocolate mousse, quite delicious.

Preparation time about 15 to 20 minutes

3½-oz (100-g) bar plain chocolate
1 level tablespoon cocoa
1 level teaspoon instant coffee powder
2 tablespoons water
8 egg whites
3 oz (75 g) caster sugar

Break the chocolate into squares, place in a bowl and stand over a pan of gently simmering water. Mix together the cocoa, instant coffee and water and add to the melted chocolate and beat together until creamy.

Whisk the egg whites using an electric hand or rotary whisk until stiff, and then whisk in the caster sugar a teaspoonful at a time, whisking all the while on maximum speed. Fold in the chocolate mixture until absorbed and the mixture is smooth.

Pour into a strengthened straight sided glass bowl, about 2 pints (1 litre) capacity, or fill 6 to 8 ramekin dishes. Cover and store in the freezer for up to 10 days (after this the mousse begins to shrink down a little from the dish). Serve still frozen with single cream.

Serves 6 to 8

Chocolate Whip

A tasty chocolate whip that is made with milk and evaporated milk instead of the usual cream. If liked decorate with swirls of cream and grated chocolate.

Preparation time about 30 minutes

½ oz (12.5 g) gelatine
3 tablespoons cold water
3 level tablespoons cocoa
4 level tablespoons caster sugar
a few drops of vanilla essence
¾ pint (450 ml) milk
1 egg, separated
1 small 6-oz (196-g) can evaporated milk, chilled

Place the gelatine in a small bowl or cup with the water and leave to stand.

Put the cocoa, sugar and vanilla essence in a saucepan, mix well, and then gradually blend in the milk and egg yolk. Bring to the boil, stirring, and simmer for a minute. Remove from the heat and stir in the gelatine until it has dissolved. Turn into a cold bowl and leave until partially set.

Whisk the evaporated milk until thick and whisk the egg white until stiff, and fold both into the chocolate mixture. Turn into a glass dish and leave to set.

Serves 6

Pots au Chocolat

One of the easiest chocolate puds. Allow 1 egg per person and always serve in very tiny pots, demi-tasse coffee cups or ramekins. Very rich, and you can, if you like, add a couple of tablespoons of rum or brandy.

Preparation time about 10 minutes

6 oz (175 g) plain chocolate
6 eggs, separated
2 tablespoons thick double cream

Put the chocolate and egg yolks in a bowl over a pan of hot water and leave to melt, stirring occasionally. Remove from the heat.

Whisk the egg whites until stiff and then fold into the chocolate mixture. Pour into 6 small pots and then leave in a cool place until set.

Just before serving top each with a dollop of cream, accompanied by sweet biscuits.

Serves 6

St Andrew's Layer

This is an easy cold pudding, that tastes good and is very rich.

Preparation time about 10 minutes

4 oz (100 g) fresh white or brown breadcrumbs
3 oz (75 g) demerara sugar
8 level tablespoons drinking chocolate
2 level tablespoons instant coffee
½ pint (300 ml) double cream
¼ pint (150 ml) single cream
2 oz (50 g) plain chocolate, coarsely grated

Place the breadcrumbs, sugar, drinking chocolate and coffee in a bowl and mix thoroughly.

Put the creams in another bowl and whisk together until they form soft peaks.

Put half the cream in the base of a 2-pint (a good litre) shallow dish, cover with the chocolate crumbs and then the remaining cream. Smooth the top and leave in the refrigerator for at least 6 hours. Cover the top with grated chocolate just before serving.

Serves 6

Chocolate Creams

Deliciously rich and so simple to make. I like to leave them overnight in the refrigerator, but if you make them early in the day they are ready to serve for dinner.

Preparation time about 5 minutes

> 5-oz (150-g) bar plain chocolate
> ½ pint (300 ml) double cream
> 1 egg
> a few drops of vanilla essence

Break the bar of chocolate into pieces and then place in a blender. Put the cream in a small saucepan and bring to the boil, pour into the blender, cover and switch on and run the machine until the chocolate has melted and the mixture is smooth.

Add the egg and a few drops of vanilla essence and blend again.

Divide the mixture between small dishes or ramekins – small because it is so rich. When set the mixture has the consistency of a smooth chocolate truffle.

Serves 6

Chocolate Trifle

A nice easy trifle that all the family will enjoy.

Preparation time about 15 minutes

> *1 chocolate Swiss Roll*
> *14½-oz (397-g) can pear halves*
> *4 level tablespoons custard powder*
> *2 level tablespoons drinking chocolate*
> *2 level tablespoons caster sugar*
> *1 pint (600 ml) milk*
> *¼ pint (150 ml) whipping cream*
> *chocolate vermicelli*

Cut the Swiss roll into 10 slices and place in a glass serving dish. Pour over the juice from the can of pears and then cut each piece of pear in half and put on top of the cake.

Put the custard powder, drinking chocolate and sugar in a bowl and stir in a little milk to make a smooth paste. Bring the remaining milk to the boil and pour onto the mixture, stirring well. Return to the saucepan and boil for a minute, stirring. Remove from the heat, turn into a bowl and whisk until cold and the custard is light and creamy. Pour over the fruit and leave to set.

Whisk the whipping cream until thick and forms soft peaks, spread over the trifle, and then sprinkle with chocolate vermicelli just before serving.

Serves 6

Chocolate Log

Very popular in our house. If time allows I like to leave overnight to firm up in the refrigerator.

Preparation time about 20 minutes

1 packet 8 trifle sponge cakes
4 oz (100 g) butter
2 oz (50 g) light soft brown sugar
2 oz (50 g) ground almonds
4 oz (100 g) plain chocolate cake covering
6-oz (196-g) can evaporated milk, chilled
¼ pint (150 ml) whipping cream
chocolate buttons to decorate

Line a 2–lb (900-g) loaf tin with foil. Take 5 of the sponge cakes, split in half horizontally and place 5 pieces in the base of the tin. Take the remaining 3 sponge cakes and make into crumbs in a blender or processor.

Cream the butter and sugar together until soft and then add the ground almonds and cake crumbs.

Break the cake covering into pieces, place in a bowl and stand over a pan of hot water. Leave to melt, then beat into the butter mixture. Whisk the evaporated milk until very thick and then beat a quarter into the chocolate mixture and carefully fold in the remaining evaporated milk.

Turn into the tin and then cover with the remaining 5 pieces of trifle sponge cake. Leave to harden in the refrigerator for at least 6 hours. Turn out onto a serving dish and peel off the foil.

Whisk the cream until thick and then use to cover the chocolate log. Decorate with chocolate buttons.

Serves 6 to 8

Chocolate Heaven

So easy to make and so good to eat, this is rather rich so it can be cut thinly to serve about 8 people. It may be stored in the freezer, then thawed and coated with the chocolate icing.

Preparation time about 10 minutes

7-oz (200-g) packet plain cooking chocolate
2 oz (50 g) butter
6-oz (196-g) can condensed milk
5 oz (150 g) rich tea biscuits
1 oz (25 g) raisins

Break half the chocolate into small pieces and place in a saucepan with the butter and condensed milk and heat through gently, stirring until the chocolate has melted and blended with the butter and milk. Remove the pan from the heat, break the biscuits into small pieces and stir into the chocolate with the raisins.

Line a 1-lb (450-g) loaf tin with a piece of foil and pour in the biscuit mixture, pack down well and then leave in the refrigerator for several hours until set. Turn it out onto a serving dish.

Break the remaining chocolate into pieces and place in a bowl over a pan of hot water and leave until melted, then spoon over the chocolate loaf and leave to set. When firm serve cut in slices.

Serves 8

Right: Apricot Creams (page 87).

Pineapple Refrigerator Cake

The easiest way to line a loaf tin with foil is first to turn the loaf tin upside down, then mould the foil over the top of the tin making a foil tin shape. Remove the foil, turn the loaf the right way up and slip the foil shape inside pressing against the tin to make it slightly smaller.

Preparation time about 15 to 20 minutes

6 oz (175 g) plain chocolate
8-oz (227-g) can pineapple rings, drained
8 oz (225 g) hard margarine such as Echo
6 oz (175 g) icing sugar, sieved
2 tablespoons golden syrup
12 oz (350 g) digestive biscuits, crushed
a little whipped cream to decorate

Line a 2-lb (900-g) loaf tin with foil. Break the chocolate into pieces, place in a bowl and stand over a saucepan of hot water until melted. Spread half of the chocolate over the base of the tin.

Place one pineapple ring on one side for decoration and then finely chop the remainder. Cream 2 oz (50 g) of the margarine with the icing sugar in a bowl until light and soft, and then stir in the chopped pineapple.

Melt the remaining margarine in a saucepan with the golden syrup, remove from the heat, add the biscuits and stir well to mix. Spread half of this mixture over the chocolate in the tin, pressing down well. On top of this spread the pineapple cream and then the remaining biscuit mixture. Carefully spoon over the rest of the melted chocolate.

Refrigerate for about 6 hours or until set. Then turn out onto a serving dish and peel off the foil. Decorate with whipped cream and the remaining pineapple ring cut in segments.

Serves 8

Left: Exotic Fruit Salad (page 101).

Chocolate Rum Charlotte

If rum isn't a top favourite, dip the sponge fingers in orange juice (the fresh variety you buy in cartons for breakfast).

Preparation time about 30 minutes

  2 tablespoons rum
  2 tablespoons water
  about 27 sponge fingers

For the mousse
  4 oz (100 g) plain chocolate
  3 eggs
  6 oz (175 g) soft unsalted butter
  5 oz (150 g) caster sugar
  ¼ pint (150 ml) whipping cream

Line a 2-lb (900-g) loaf tin with foil. Mix the rum and water together in a saucer. Dip each sponge finger sugar-side down in the rum mixture, and arrange 9 to 10 fingers sugar side down on the base of the tin. Cut the remaining sponge fingers in half and dip sugar side down in the rum mixture and stand, sugar side out, around the tin.

For the mousse, break the chocolate into pieces and place in a small bowl over a pan of simmering water and allow to melt slowly. Separate the eggs, place the whites in a large bowl and put the yolks in a bowl with the butter and sugar and beat well until creamy. Stir in the cooled chocolate, which should still be runny.

Whisk the egg whites until stiff but not dry and fold gently into the chocolate mixture using a metal spoon. Turn into the loaf tin and smooth the top. Chill overnight.

Next day turn out onto a serving dish. Remove the foil. Whisk the cream until thick, then pipe rosettes on the charlotte.

Serves 8

Canaletto Dessert Cake

This is a delicious rich chocolate cake, a great favourite on a special occasion such as a birthday. Use the ends of the sponge fingers in a trifle or fruit fool.

Preparation time about 15 minutes

1 packet (16) sponge fingers
4 oz (100 g) unsalted butter
4 oz (100 g) caster sugar
2 eggs
3½-oz (100-g) bar plain or milk chocolate
1½ tablespoons coffee essence
¼ pint (150 ml) whipping cream
Maltesers to decorate

Trim the rounded ends off each sponge finger and use to cover the base of a 7-inch (17.5-cm) square tin with a loose base.

Cream the butter and sugar together in a large bowl until very soft. Separate the eggs and beat the yolks into the creamed mixture.

Break the chocolate into small pieces and place in a bowl with the coffee essence, stand over a pan of hot water and heat very gently until the chocolate has melted and is smooth. Stir into the butter and sugar mixture and mix throughly.

Whisk the egg whites with an electric or hand rotary whisk until stiff and then fold into the chocolate mixture. Turn into the tin, smooth the top, and leave in the refrigerator for several hours or until firm.

Turn out onto a serving dish so that the sponge fingers are at the top. Whisk the cream until thick and firm enough to pipe and use to decorate the cake by marking into eight portions. Decorate with the Maltesers.

Serves 8

Chocolate Celebration Cake

This is such an easy cake when made in the processor or blender, and it makes a lovely moist pudding. Keep any left-overs in the refrigerator and serve at tea. (*Illustrated on the jacket.*)

Preparation time about 5 minutes
Cooking time about 40 minutes

6½ oz (190 g) self-raising flour
5 oz (150 g) caster sugar
2 eggs
¼ pint (150 ml) oil
¼ pint (150 ml) milk
1 teaspoon bicarbonate of soda
2 tablespoons golden syrup
2 tablespoons cocoa, sieved

Filling and topping
½ pint (300 ml) double cream
chocolate flake or grated chocolate

Heat the oven to 325°F, 160°C, gas mark 3. Grease and line with greased greaseproof paper 2× 8 inch (20 cm) sandwich tins.

Blend all the cake ingredients together until smooth. Pour into the tins and bake in the oven for 40 minutes or until the cake springs back when pressed and comes away from the sides of the tin. Cool and then remove the paper.

Whisk the cream for the filling and topping until thick and then use half to sandwich the cakes together. Spread the remaining cream over the top of the cake and sprinkle with chocolate flake or grated chocolate.

Serves 6 to 8

Chocolate Freezer Cake

This cake is very moist and freezes well.

Preparation time about 15 minutes
Cooking time about 40 minutes

11 oz (325 g) caster sugar
6 tablespoons water
3 oz (75 g) cocoa powder
¼ pint (150 ml) milk
8 oz (225 g) butter
4 eggs, separated
8 oz (225 g) self-raising flour
2 level teaspoons baking powder
apricot jam
½ pint (300 ml) double cream
icing sugar

Heat the oven to 350°F, 180°C, gas mark 4. Line 2×8-inch (20-cm) deep sandwich tins with greased greaseproof paper.

Put 3 oz (75 g) of the sugar in a saucepan with the water and cocoa and mix to a thick paste. Cook gently until the mixture is thick and shiny. Stir in the milk and leave to cool.

Cream the butter with the remaining sugar until the mixture is pale and fluffy. Beat in the egg yolks with the chocolate mixture. Sift the flour with the baking powder and fold into the mixture. Whisk the egg whites until stiff and then fold carefully into the chocolate mixture. Divide between the cake tins and bake in the oven for about 40 minutes or until the cake springs back when lightly pressed with a fingertip. Turn out cakes, peel off paper and cool on a wire rack.

Whisk the cream until thick. Split both sponges in half horizontally and sandwich them all together with apricot jam and cream. Dredge with sieved icing sugar.

Serves 8

Milk Chocolate Cheesecake

This doesn't in fact use milk chocolate but it tastes as though it does. Make a day ahead as this is a soft cheesecake relying on the chocolate to set it and is best left overnight in the refrigerator before turning out.

Preparation time about 20 minutes

12 oz (350 g) cream cheese
4 oz (100 g) caster sugar
3 eggs, separated
7-oz (200-g) bar plain chocolate
¾ pint (450 ml) double cream
4 oz (100 g) digestive biscuits, crushed
2 oz (50 g) butter, melted
a few chocolate buttons to decorate

Line the base of an 8-inch (20-cm) loose bottomed cake tin with a piece of greaseproof paper. Place the cream cheese in a large roomy bowl with the caster sugar and beat well until creamy. Then beat in the egg yolks. Break the chocolate into small pieces, put in a bowl, and stand over a pan of hot water until melted. Leave to cool slightly then beat into the cheese mixture.

Lightly whisk the cream until it forms soft peaks and then whisk the egg whites until stiff. Fold the cream into the chocolate mixture and then lastly fold in the egg whites. Turn the mixture into the tin and smooth the top.

Mix the biscuit crumbs with the melted butter and then spread over the top of the cheese cake. Leave in the refrigerator for a day.

Turn out onto a flat serving dish so that the biscuit base is at the bottom, carefully peel off the greaseproof paper and decorate the top of the cheesecake with chocolate buttons.

Serves 8

Chocolate Tiffin

Expensive, but divine with coffee instead of a pudding.

Preparation time about 12 to 15 minutes

4 oz (100 g) hard margarine such as Echo
3 level tablespoons golden syrup
1 oz (25 g) drinking chocolate or cocoa
2 oz (50 g) glacé cherries, chopped
8 oz (225 g) digestive biscuits, crushed

Topping
6 oz (175 g) plain or milk chocolate

Line a 7×11 inch (17.5×27.5 cm) tin with foil.

Place the margarine, golden syrup and drinking chocolate in a pan and heat until the butter has melted. Remove from the heat, stir in the glacé cherries and crushed biscuits, and mix thoroughly. Turn into the tin, press down firmly and then leave in the refrigerator until firm.

Break the chocolate into small pieces and place in a bowl over a pan of hot water until melted and then spread over the biscuit base and leave until firm. Remove the foil and then cut into 16 pieces.

Makes 16 pieces of tiffin

CHILDREN'S CHOICE

Children love all kinds of pudding. Let them make their own and you may be surprised by their ingenuity.

Top favourite is ice cream (see the next chapter). Children are perfectly happy with the bought variety, happier probably than with an elaborate home-made kind. I find that what they like best is plain vanilla flavour with *plenty* of topping. Sauces for ice cream can be bought, and are inclined to be expensive, or you can make them at home – chocolate and butterscotch. My daughter Annabel makes her own and keeps a supply in the freezer to be issued to her friends during the school holidays.

All kinds of jelly are popular, and the children like to make theirs themselves. Provide them, if you can, with individual fancy jelly moulds. This avoids arguments about who gets the rabbit's face or whatever.

Any pudding with chocolate in it is guaranteed success (see the preceding chapter). Mousses and whips of various kinds go down very well and canned fruit, particularly peaches and pineapple, with cream, is a certain success. Frosty carnival pudding made with rice crispies is much in demand, as well.

As children grow older they seem to turn to the more traditional puddings, the baked and steamed ones, the fruit tarts and jam rolypolys that bring a meal to such a satisfying end.

Framfield Crème

If you are making this for children and you have some bought vanilla ice cream in the freezer, soften a family block and use instead of whipped cream and serve at once. Apart from it being more reasonable, I find young children prefer ice cream to cream. I have made this with different fruit purées: gooseberry is my favourite, but then I use only white marshmallows.

Preparation time about 5 minutes

4 oz (100 g) marshmallows
¼ pint (150 ml) fresh raspberry or strawberry purée
½ pint (300 ml) whipping cream, whipped
about 1 oz (25 g) caster sugar
a few fresh raspberries or strawberries for decoration

First snip each marshmallow into about 6 pieces in a largish bowl, add the fruit purée and cream and fold together. Sweeten to taste with a little caster sugar.

Turn into 6 glasses or ramekin dishes and decorate with fresh raspberries or strawberries. Chill before serving if time allows.

Serves 6

Citrus Crunch

Older children can quite easily make this pudding. An ideal dish to produce on Mother's birthday.

Preparation time about 15 minutes

3 oz (75 g) butter
8 oz (225 g) fresh brown breadcrumbs
1½ oz (40 g) demerara sugar
2 oz (50 g) plain chocolate, grated
11-oz (312-g) can mandarin oranges, drained
½ pint (300 ml) double cream
grated rind and juice of half a lemon

Heat the butter in a frying pan, add the breadcrumbs and fry, turning continually until crisp. Turn out of the pan, leave to cool and then stir in the demerara sugar and grated chocolate.

Reserve 8 mandarin orange segments and then purée the remainder in a blender or processor. Turn into a bowl with the double cream and lemon rind and juice and then whisk until thick.

Place alternate layers of breadcrumbs and cream mixture in 4 individual glasses, starting with crumbs and ending with cream and making 4 layers in all. Decorate each glass with 2 mandarin segments and if liked sprinkle with a little extra grated chocolate.

Serves 4

Pineapple Whip

This is a simple type of sweet that children can make for themselves. The ideal pudding to make for a surprise dinner for Mum!

Preparation time about 5 minutes

15-oz (425-g) can pineapple pieces, drained
3 oz (75 g) white marshmallows
¼ pint (150 ml) double cream
1½ level tablespoons caster sugar
1 tablespoon lemon juice

Place all the ingredients in a blender or processor and run until smooth and blended. Turn into 4 small dishes or glasses and chill in the refrigerator until required.

Serve with shortbread biscuits (see page 188).

Serves 4

Rice Compote

This is one of those nice, easy recipes that children like to make. If raisins are not too popular, try glacé cherries or dates, roughly chopped.

Preparation time about 15 minutes

2 oz (50 g) seedless raisins
2 tablespoons fresh orange juice
15½-oz (439-g) can creamed rice
¼ pint (150 ml) whipping cream
2 large chocolate flake bars

Place the raisins in a bowl, pour over the orange juice and leave to stand for 10 minutes, stirring occasionally. Then stir in the can of creamed rice. Lightly whisk the cream until thick and it holds a soft peak. Crumble up one of the chocolate bars and stir into the rice mixture with the cream.

Turn into 4 small serving dishes or glasses and just before serving sprinkle the remaining flake on top.

Serves 4

Trifle

Children sometimes like to make a special pudding as a treat for their parents. Let them try this – it's so easy and it tastes and looks good.

Preparation time about 10 minutes

3 trifle sponge cakes or 2 oz (50 g) stale fatless sponge cake
2 oz (50 g) macaroons (see page 189)
15-oz (425-g) can white peaches or other fruit
2 to 3 tablespoons sweet sherry
½ pint (300 ml) double or whipping cream
orange and lemon slices to decorate

Break the sponge cakes into pieces and place in a serving dish with the macaroons. Pour over the peaches and their syrup, with the sherry.

Whisk the cream until thick and forms soft peaks and then spread over the top of the trifle. Leave in a cool place until required.

Just before serving decorate with orange and lemon slices.

Serves 4 to 6

Chocolate Ice Cream Log

This is a perfect pudding for children to make themselves. My children also like it made with an ordinary jam-filled Swiss roll, sandwiched with slices of raspberry ripple ice cream.

Preparation time about 5 minutes

1 chocolate Swiss roll
6 slices vanilla ice cream
½ pint (300 ml) whipping cream
chocolate vermicelli or grated chocolate
a few chopped nuts

Cut the Swiss roll into 7 even slices, then sandwich back together on a serving dish with a portion of ice cream between each slice of roll, keeping a slice of Swiss roll at each end.

Whisk the cream until thick and then spread evenly over the cake and ice cream. Sprinkle thickly with chocolate vermicelli or grated chocolate and if liked a few chopped nuts.

Serves 6

Lemon Passion

A simple good weekday pudding that many children like making.

Preparation time about 15 minutes

> *half packet lemon jelly*
> *¼ pint (150 ml) double cream*
> *½ pint (300 ml) natural yogurt*

Place the jelly in a measure and make up to ¼ pint (150 ml) with boiling water, and stir until dissolved. Leave to get cold, then turn into a bowl.

Whisk the cream until it forms soft peaks. Stir the yogurt into the jelly and fold in the cream.

Turn into 4 individual glasses or dishes and leave to set.

Serves 4

St Clement's Jelly

Jelly is a great favourite with all ages. To speed up making jelly use ice cubes or include frozen fruit like raspberries or strawberries. (*Illustrated on the jacket.*)

Preparation time about 30 minutes

half packet lemon jelly
half packet orange jelly
11-oz (312-g) can mandarin oranges

Make up each jelly separately following the instructions on the packet, but when making up the orange jelly use the juice from the mandarin oranges.

Run a little cold water around a 1-pint (600-ml) jelly mould and then pour in the orange jelly and leave to set. Then pour over the lemon jelly and let this set too.

Turn out onto a serving dish and surround with mandarin oranges.

Serves 4 to 6

Raspberry Jelly

Preparation time about 30 minutes

1 packet raspberry jelly
ice cubes
about 6 oz (175 g) frozen raspberries

Make the raspberry jelly using ½ pint (300 ml) boiling water as directed on the packet. Then add ¼ pint (150 ml) cold water and about 12 ice cubes, stirring well until dissolved and the jelly measures 1 pint (600 ml).

Stir in the raspberries and then turn into a serving dish and leave to set. Serve with thin cream.

Serves 4 to 6

Orange Jelly Creams

It is great fun decorating these jellies, and you could let each child decorate their own.

Preparation time about 15 minutes

1 packet of orange jelly
½ pint (300 ml) boiling water
11-oz (312-g) can mandarin oranges
1 large can condensed milk
2 tablespoons lemon juice
angelica for decoration

Dissolve the jelly in the boiling water. Drain the mandarins and add the juice to the jelly to make up to ¾ pint (450 ml). Leave on one side to cool. Whisk in the condensed milk, then stir in about half the mandarins, leaving the remainder for decoration. Stir in the lemon juice.

Divide the mixture between 6 individual glasses or dishes and leave to set. Decorate each cream jelly with the remaining mandarin oranges and strips of angelica.

Serves 6

Butterscotch Cheat Flan

Leave off the nuts for the very young and use all digestive biscuits, for the crust. Very nice if you slice a banana into the crust before adding the whip.

Preparation time about 10 minutes

Biscuit crust
    2 oz (50 g) digestive biscuits
    2 oz (50 g) ginger biscuits
    2 oz (50 g) butter
    1 oz (25 g) soft brown sugar

Filling
    8 fluid oz (250 ml) milk
    2.5-oz (72-g) packet butterscotch flavour dessert whip

    walnuts to decorate

Put the biscuits in a polythene bag and crush with a rolling pin. Melt the butter in a small pan, add the sugar and stir in the biscuit crumbs and mix well. Turn into an 8-inch (20-cm) flan dish and press into shape around the base and sides with the back of a spoon.

For the filling make up according to the directions on the packet but using only 8 fluid oz (250 ml) milk. Turn into the flan case and leave in a cool place to set. When ready to serve, decorate with walnuts.

Serves 6

Frosty Carnival

This is an exciting way of using ice cream. The crunchy flan base can be made in advance and kept in foil or a tin until required.

Preparation time about 15 minutes

Base
    2 oz (50 g) butter
    4 oz (100 g) golden syrup
    2 oz (50 g) soft brown sugar
    4 oz (100 g) marshmallows
    3 oz (75 g) rice krispies

Sauce
    4 oz (100 g) caramel toffees
    4 tablespoons milk

Filling
    17 fluid oz (500 ml) block vanilla ice cream

Grease an 8-inch (20-cm) flan ring and place on a greased baking tray.

Put the butter, syrup and sugar into a large saucepan and heat gently until the butter has melted, and then boil the mixture for 1 minute. Remove the pan from the heat, add the marshmallows and stir until melted, then mix in the rice krispies thoroughly. Press into the flan ring, using the back of a spoon, then leave in a cool place to set.

Place the ingredients for the sauce in a basin over a pan of hot water. Leave to melt, stirring occasionally.

Just before serving, put spoonfuls of ice cream onto the flan and pour over the caramel sauce. Serve at once.

Serves 6

Pineapple Upside-Down Pudding

My daughter makes this whenever the oven is on, or she can get into the kitchen. It never fails and always looks good. Serve with custard or vanilla ice cream.

Preparation time about 10 minutes
Baking time about 25 minutes

Sponge
   3 oz (75 g) self-raising flour
   3 oz (75 g) soft margarine
   3 oz (75 g) caster sugar
   1 egg, beaten
   1 tablespoon pineapple juice
   ½ level teaspoon baking powder

Topping
   8-oz (227-g) can pineapple slices, drained
   2 glacé cherries, halved
   2 oz (50 g) light soft brown sugar

Heat the oven to 375°F, 190°C, gas mark 5. Well butter a 7-inch (17.5-cm) round cake tin.

Place all the sponge ingredients in a bowl and beat well for about 2 minutes or until well blended.

Place 4 pineapple rings in the base of the tin and put a halved cherry in the centre of each ring, cut side uppermost. Sprinkle over the brown sugar. Spread sponge mixture over pineapple and smooth the top.

Bake in the oven for about 25 minutes until the cake is well risen and a golden brown colour and the centre will spring back when lightly pressed with the finger. Leave to cool in the tin for about 10 minutes, then turn out, pineapple uppermost, and serve warm.

Serves 4

Apple Snowballs

Baked apples with a meringue topping and jammy filling. A good way of using up egg whites.

Preparation time about 10 minutes
Cooking time about 25 minutes

4 medium sized cooking apples
2 egg whites
3 oz (75 g) caster sugar
raspberry jam

Heat the oven to 350°F, 180°C, gas mark 4.

Wash the apples and then peel and core and place in an ovenproof dish. Cover with a lid or foil and bake in the oven for about 15 minutes or until they are soft when prodded with a knife or skewer.

Meanwhile whisk the egg whites with a rotary or electric hand whisk until stiff and then whisk in the sugar a teaspoonful at a time.

Remove the apples from the oven and fill the centres with raspberry jam. Pile the meringue over the apples and then return to the oven for a futher 10 minutes or until they are crisp and lightly brown.

Serve at once.

Serves 4

Cherry and Maple Sponge

I'm not a great one for packet sponges but they are better served hot than cold. Serve with extra maple syrup or custard.

Preparation time about 10 minutes
Cooking time about 1 hour

2 tablespoons maple syrup
2 oz (50 g) glacé cherries
8-oz (225-g) packet luxury sponge mix
1 egg

Put the maple syrup in a greased 1½-pint (900-ml) basin. Cut the cherries in halves and then halve again and place in the bowl on top of the maple syrup.

Make up the packet of sponge mix, using the egg as directed on the packet, pour into the basin and cover with a lid of foil.

Have ready a saucepan of boiling water, or steamer with lower half filled with boiling water. Put in the pudding and steam or simmer for about 1 hour or until the centre of the sponge will spring back when lightly pressed.

Turn out onto a warm serving plate.

Serves 4

Butterscotch Sauce

This sauce is always very popular in our house. Delicious hot over ice cream and bananas. Any spare can be stored in a screw-topped jar in the refrigerator. It can be served cold thereafter, or reheated in a bowl over a pan of simmering water.

Preparation time about 10 minutes

2 oz (50 g) margarine
6 oz (175 g) demerara sugar
6-oz (170-g) can evaporated milk

Melt the margarine in a small saucepan, add the sugar and stir until dissolved, then boil gently for 3 minutes.

Remove the pan from the heat and stir in the evaporated milk, return to the heat and bring back to the boil, stirring until well blended.

Serve either hot or cold.

Chocolate Toffee Sauce

Make this up and keep in the refrigerator until required and then warm to serve over ice cream.

Preparation time about 5 minutes

12 oz (350 g) soft brown sugar
4 level tablespoons cocoa powder
4 oz (100 g) hard margarine, such as Echo
4 tablespoons golden syrup
¼ pint (150 ml) milk

Put all the ingredients in a saucepan and heat through gently, stirring constantly, until the sugar has dissolved and the margarine has melted. Boil rapidly for a minute. Then remove the pan from the heat and the sauce is ready to serve.

Or you could leave it to cool slightly in the pan and then turn into a container and store covered in the refrigerator.

FROZEN PUDDINGS

Ice cream is a fast pudding if you make it in advance and freeze it ready for use. If you are really pushed for time, scoop out the ice cream from its container before the meal begins and pile it into a wide flat serving dish (I prefer glass dishes for ice cream), or into individual glasses. Keep it frozen until you are ready, then top it with home-made sauce or decorate it with fruit or in any other way you choose, and serve it with sponge fingers or almond biscuits.

When you are making ice cream always make an extra amount to keep in the freezer. Use it up within about 3 months. There are any amount of ice cream recipes and most cooks have their favourites. Mine is rich but not over expensive and its great advantage is that it does not have to be whisked halfway through its freezing time. It is not based on custard which can curdle, or on too much liquid which can crystallise. Briefly, I separate the eggs and make a meringue with the whites. Into this I beat the yolks and add flavouring – fruit, chocolate, coffee or whatever. In short, I make a light and airy mousse without too much liquid. Then I simply freeze it.

Try a sorbet, they are very easy to make. You simply make a fruit fool, fold in egg whites and freeze. In the days when our ancestors – those of them who could afford to – indulged in enormous banquets of innumerable courses, sorbets were produced at half time to clear the diners' palates for the next rich round of dishes. Today we keep sorbets for the end of a meal and deliciously light and refreshing they are, too. Make them with fruit – orange, lemon, lime, grapefruit – or for a special treat with liqueur. Serve them in individual glasses, ice-cold and frosty from the freezer.

Peach Melba

A very special way of serving ice cream, it is important to use fresh peaches and raspberries and a good quality vanilla ice cream.

Preparation time about 15 minutes

4 fresh peaches
8 oz (225 g) caster sugar
1 pint (600 ml) water
8 oz (225 g) fresh raspberries
4 oz (100 g) icing sugar
vanilla ice cream (see page 156)
¼ pint (150 ml) double cream, whipped
finely slivered almonds

Peel, halve and stone the peaches. Put the caster sugar and water in a large shallow pan and simmer together, stirring occasionally until the sugar has dissolved. Put the peaches in a single layer in the pan and simmer gently for about 10 minutes. Then remove the pan from the heat and leave the peaches to cool in the syrup. When quite cold, lift out the peaches with a slotted spoon.

For the sauce, place the raspberries in an electric blender for a few seconds with the icing sugar until smooth and then sieve into a bowl to remove all the pips.

Place a portion of ice cream in 4 sundae glasses and arrange 2 peach halves in the dish. Pour over some raspberry sauce and pipe a swirl of cream on top. Sprinkle with almonds and serve.

Serves 4

Vanilla Ice Cream

This is an ideal stand-by to keep in the deep freeze. Use as a base for sundaes or parfaits (see knickerbocker glory, page 172), or serve with hot puddings and pies instead of custard or cream.

Preparation time about 5 to 8 minutes

> *4 eggs*
> *4 oz (100 g) caster sugar*
> *½ pint (300 ml) double cream*

Separate the eggs. Place the yolks in a small bowl and whisk until well blended. Using a rotary or electric hand whisk, whisk the egg whites until stiff, then whisk in the sugar a teaspoonful at a time. Whisk the cream until it forms soft peaks, then fold into the egg white mixture with the egg yolks. (Add any extras at this stage – see opposite.)

Turn into a 2½-pint (1.4-litre) container, cover and freeze until solid. Remove from the freezer and leave to stand at room temperature for 5 to 10 minutes before serving.

Serves 8 to 10

Tutti Fruiti

Add 4 oz (100 g) chopped glacé pineapple, raisins, dried apricots, cherries and angelica soaked overnight in 4 tablespoons of brandy to plump them up. Fold into the basic ice cream recipe just before freezing. Serve with almond biscuits, a swirl of cream and a sprinkling of nuts.

Blackcurrant Ice Cream

Add about 6 tablespoonfuls of blackcurrant cordial (Ribena) to the basic recipe.

Coffee and Brandy Ice Cream

Add 2 tablespoons coffee essence and 2 tablespoons brandy to the basic ice cream.

Fresh Lemon Ice Cream

Add the grated rind and juice of 2 lemons to the basic ice cream.

Mango Ice Cream

Add the lightly mashed flesh of a peeled and stoned mango to the basic ice cream.

Chocolate Ice Cream

Add 4 oz (100 g) melted plain chocolate to the egg yolks in the basic recipe. Use chilled evaporated milk instead of double cream.

Plum Ice Cream

Add about ¼ pint (150 ml) thick plum purée to the basic ice cream, which makes a very pretty deep pink colour, and gives it an unusual flavour.

Quick Blender Ice Cream

This is a less rich ice cream than our basic vanilla ice, but is easy to make from ingredients in the store cupboard. Several variations are given below. Alternatively, pour on a fruit topping, and serve with fruit. (*See picture facing page 161.*)

Preparation time about 15 minutes

1 level teaspoon powdered gelatine
¾ pint (450 ml) milk
1 level tablespoon custard powder
3 level tablespoons caster sugar
4 oz (100 g) unsalted butter, cut in small pieces
1 teaspoon vanilla essence

Put the gelatine in a small basin with a tablespoon of milk. Make the custard with the remaining milk, custard powder and sugar, then pour into the blender and add the gelatine, butter and vanilla essence. Blend for 30 seconds.

Leave to cool slightly then pour into a refrigerator tray and freeze until just firm. Return mixture to blender to re-whip then re-freeze until really firm.

Serves 6

Peach Ice Cream

Add 4 fresh peaches, puréed with 2 tablespoons of caster sugar, to the completed mixture. Then freeze until firm and re-whip as above. Omit vanilla essence.

Chocolate Mint Ice Cream

Add 4 oz (100 g) plain chocolate, broken into squares to the hot custard in the blender with about 5 drops of peppermint essence and some green colouring. Blend for 30 seconds as above. Omit the vanilla essence.

Strawberry Ice Cream

Coarsely chop 4 oz (100 g) fresh strawberries with about 3 tablespoons caster sugar and then stir into the completed blended mixture. Omit the vanilla essence.

Banana and Praline Ice Cream

Melt 1 oz (25 g) unsalted butter with 3 oz (75 g) caster sugar and stir until light brown. Add 4 oz (100 g) blanched chopped almonds and stir until they are also light brown. Spoon onto a buttered baking sheet and when cool and hard, crush finely. Make the ice cream as in the basic recipe and add the crushed praline with 4 puréed bananas to the completed mixture. Omit the vanilla essence. Put in the freezer for 2 hours and stir every 30 minutes.

Grapefruit Sorbet

Serve piled up in glasses, and decorate with lemon balm or mint sprigs.

Preparation time about 10 minutes

finely grated rind and strained juice from 2 grapefruit
2 tablespoons runny honey
¼ pint (150 ml) double cream
2 egg whites
3 oz (75 g) caster sugar

Mix the rind, grapefruit juice and honey together. Whisk the cream until thick and will hold a soft peak then beat in the grapefruit mixture.

Whisk the egg whites with an electric hand whisk or a rotary whisk until stiff and then whisk in the sugar, a teaspoonful at a time. Fold into the cream.

Turn into an ice cube tray and leave in the deep freeze for 2 hours, then remove and beat well with a wooden spoon and return to the dish for a further 4 hours.

If liked the mixture can be beaten again, and then covered and used as required.

Serves 4

Right: Hot Apple Scone (page 117).

Orange Sorbet

The frozen concentrated orange is extremely good. They say that each can contains 11 oranges, so it's good value, too.

Preparation time about 10 minutes

3 oz (75 g) caster sugar
½ pint (300 ml) water
6½-fluid oz (184-g) can concentrated frozen orange juice, undiluted
1 egg white

Put the sugar and water in a pan and heat slowly until the sugar has dissolved. Leave to cool and then stir in the orange juice and blend well. Pour into a 1-pint (600-ml) container. Freeze for about half an hour or until barely firm, then turn into a bowl and mash down.

Whisk the egg white until stiff and then fold into the orange mixture, return to the freezer in the container with a lid on, and then freeze until firm.

Leave to thaw in the refrigerator for 30 minutes before serving.

Serves 4

Left: Quick Blender Ice Creams (page 158).

Pineapple Sorbet

Very refreshing at the end of a meal.

Preparation time about 10 minutes

15½-oz (439-g) can pineapple pieces
6 oz (175 g) granulated sugar
grated rind and juice of 1 lemon
1 level teaspoon gelatine
1 tablespoon water
2 egg whites

Drain the pineapple pieces and reserve the juice. Make the juice up to ¾ pint (450 ml) with water and put in a saucepan with the sugar. Heat gently until the sugar has dissolved, stirring occasionally. Simmer for 2 minutes and then remove from the heat and add the lemon rind and juice.

Place the gelatine and water in a small cup and leave to stand for a minute, then place in a pan of gently simmering water until dissolved. Stir into the sugar syrup.

Purée the pineapple in a processor or blender and add to the sugar syrup. Turn the mixture into a plastic container, cover and leave in the freezing compartment of the refrigerator or deep freeze until almost solid. Turn into a bowl and whisk until smooth. Whisk the egg whites until they form soft peaks and then fold into the pineapple mixture. Return to the container, cover and freeze until required.

Serves 6

Melon and Ginger Sorbet

This amount of ginger makes it quite hot, so add less if you like. There's no syrup to make in this sorbet.

Preparation time about 15 minutes

1 medium melon
juice of half a lemon
scant level teaspoon powdered ginger
4 egg whites
4 oz (100 g) caster sugar
3 to 4 tablespoons Maraschino cherries

Cut the melon in half, remove the seeds and then scoop out the flesh (keep the shells). Place flesh in a blender or processor with the lemon juice and ginger and blend until smooth.

Turn into a 3-pint (1.7-litre) container and freeze until beginning to set. Whisk the egg whites with an electric or rotary whisk until stiff and then whisk in the sugar a teaspoonful at a time.

Lightly whisk the melon mixture until broken up and then fold in the egg whites. Return to the freezer until set.

Remove from the freezer about 5 minutes before serving and spoon into the bottom half of the melon shell, top with the Maraschino cherries and then place the top of the melon shell over the sorbet. Serve at once.

Serves 6 to 8

Grand Marnier Water Ice

Use any liqueur that you have to hand – Benedictine is good – and add a little green colouring too.

Preparation time about 15 minutes

> *7 oz (200 g) granulated sugar*
> *¾ pint (450 ml) water*
> *juice of 1 lemon*
> *4 to 5 tablespoons Grand Marnier*
> *¼ pint (150 ml) double cream, whipped*

Place the sugar, water and lemon juice in a small saucepan and bring to the boil, stirring until the sugar has dissolved and then boil for 2 to 3 minutes. Remove from the heat and turn into a freezing tray or plastic container. When cold put in the coldest part of the freezer and leave until mushy.

Turn the syrup into a cold bowl and whip lightly. Whisk in the Grand Marnier and then fold in the whipped cream. Return to the freezer container, cover and freeze until firm.

When required, serve in scoops in tall glasses.

Serves 4

Scarsgrove Orange
Ice Box Cake

Ginger and orange make a good combination and this is an ideal dish to have in the deep freeze for those unexpected guests.

Preparation time about 8 minutes

2 pint (1 litre) block of vanilla ice cream
grated rind and juice of 1 orange
grated rind of 1 lemon
thin ginger biscuits
a little whipped cream
orange slices or thin slices of stem ginger

Place the contents of the ice cream container in a large bowl with the orange rind and juice and lemon rind, and mix well until blended.

Arrange some of the ginger biscuits over the base of the ice cream container, if necessary cutting to fit. Return the ice cream to the container and then cover the top with another layer of ginger biscuits. Cover, label and freeze until required.

Leave to stand at room temperature for 5 minutes then turn out onto a flat serving dish and decorate with whipped cream and orange or ginger slices.

Serves 6

Biscuit Tortoni

I like to serve this with a bowl of fresh raspberries or strawberries. It is not really an ice cream, more a frozen sweet.

Preparation time about 15 minutes

½ pint (300 ml) double cream
¼ pint (150 ml) single cream
a few drops vanilla essence
2 to 3 tablespoons sweet sherry
4 oz (100 g) icing sugar, sieved
2 egg whites
4 oz (100 g) macaroons, crushed (see page 189)

Put the creams in a bowl and whisk until thick and form soft peaks and then whisk in the vanilla essence, sherry and half the icing sugar.

Whisk the egg whites using a rotary or electric hand whisk until stiff and then whisk in the remaining icing sugar a teaspoonful at a time. Fold into the cream with the crushed macaroons.

Turn into a foil-lined 2-lb (900-g) loaf tin, cover and freeze until firm. When required leave to thaw in the refrigerator for 2 to 3 hours, then serve cut in slices. The pudding should be still chilled and firm.

Serves 8

Bombe Favorite

We used to make this at college, and it's not really an ice cream, just a frozen cream mixture. I make it in the summer when I serve it with a fresh raspberry sauce or a bowl of strawberries from the garden. It is a very good way of using up any meringues.

Preparation time about 5 minutes

3 oz (75 g) meringue shells (see page 184)
½ pint (300 ml) double cream
a little Kirsch or brandy to flavour (optional)
1 tablespoon vanilla sugar
raspberry sauce (see peach melba, page 155)

Oil a 1½-pint (900-ml) basin. Lightly crumble the meringues, but keep the pieces quite big.

Whisk the cream until thick and will hold soft peaks and then fold in the Kirsch or brandy (if used), with a little sugar and the crumbled meringues. Mix thoroughly and then turn into the basin. Cover with a lid of foil and freeze until firm.

When required, turn out onto a serving dish, leave in the refrigerator for about 5 minutes and then serve with raspberry sauce.

Serves 4 to 6

Lemon Freeze

If you like your puddings very lemony you could add the rind of a lemon to the mixture. This is the sort of pudding that I find very handy to keep in the freezer: it can be served just as it is, or is delicious served with raspberries.

Preparation time about 15 minutes

3 oz (75 g) cornflakes, crushed
3 level tablespoons caster sugar
1½ oz (40 g) butter, melted

Lemon filling
2 eggs, separated
6-oz (196-g) can condensed milk
4 tablespoons lemon juice
3 level tablespoons caster sugar

Place the cornflakes in a bowl with the caster sugar and mix well, then stir in the melted butter until thoroughly blended. Press *half* this mixture over the base of an 8-inch (20-cm) loose-bottomed cake tin.

To make the filling, beat the egg yolks until creamy and then blend in the condensed milk and lemon juice, until the mixture thickens.

Whisk the egg whites with an electric hand or rotary whisk until stiff and then whisk in the sugar a spoonful at a time. Fold into the lemon mixture and then turn into the cake tin and smooth the top. Cover with the remaining cornflake mixture, pressing lightly on top. Cover and freeze until firm.

Leave to stand at room temperature for about 5 minutes, then turn out and serve cut in wedges.

Serves 8

TEN-MINUTE PUDDINGS

These are all simple ideas, using what you have in the store cupboard or freezer. They are all quick, useful for mid-week suppers for the busy housewife who does her more ambitious cooking at weekends. Many of them are little more than a matter of assembling the ingredients you have on hand and if you keep up a good store of canned fruit, cream, yogurt, instant whips, biscuits, breadcrumbs, eggs and so on, this should present no difficulties.

Some of the ideas are as basic and easy to do as fried bananas with demerara sugar. Let the children make theirs. To keep the peace, each does his own and the last one washes the pan!

Sue Laughton's Apricot Fool

Sue suggests this when no pudding is even thought of and there's 5 minutes to go! Put a can of apricot pie filling in a processor or blender, add a can-ful of fresh milk and blend until smooth. Turn into a glass dish and serve.

Serves about 4

Coffee Cream

Put ½ pint (300 ml) thick cold custard in the processor or blender with 2 to 3 level teaspoons of instant coffee powder and run until blended. Then add ½ pint (300 ml) double cream and whizz until smooth, taste, and if liked sweeten with a little caster sugar. For a special occasion you could add a little brandy. Turn into 3 glass dishes and serve.

Serves 3

Strawberry Yogurt Fool

Stir 2 to 3 tablespoons of fruit purée such as raspberry, strawberry or blackcurrant into ¼ pint (150 ml) low fat natural yogurt to give a swirled effect. Turn into an individual dish and chill for 1 hour to allow the flavours to blend. Sprinkle with a few chopped roasted nuts.

Serves 1

Butterscotch Bananas

Slice 2 bananas and divide between 3 glasses or individual dishes. Make up a packet of butterscotch dessert whip and fold in about 2 oz (50 g) crushed nut brittle. Pile on bananas and serve in 5 minutes.

Serves 3

Creamy Blackcurrant Flan

Put ¼ pint (150 ml) double cream into a bowl and whisk until thick, then fold in a 14-oz (396-g) can blackcurrant fruit filling with a tablespoon of caster sugar to taste. Pile into a 7- to 8-inch (17.5- to 20-cm) sponge flan case and then chill well before serving.

Serves 4 to 6

Saucy Lemon Mousse

Drain the syrup from an 11-oz (312-g) can mandarin oranges and put in a saucepan with 2 teaspoons custard powder, and bring to the boil, stirring until thickened. Simmer for 1 minute, then add the mandarin oranges and mix lightly. Remove from the heat and serve either hot or cold over slices of lemon mousse.

Serves 4

Caramel Pears

Take 1 large pear per person and peel with a potato peeler. Cut into 8 wedges and remove the core. Melt about 2 oz (50 g) butter and 4 oz (100 g) demerara sugar in a frying pan, stirring gently until the sugar dissolves. Then add the pears and cook gently, turning once, for about 6 minutes, when they will be tender and the outside a pale caramel colour. Serve with a bowl of thick cream.

Caramel Apple Rings

Make and cook as above only once the apples are peeled, core and then cut each apple into 3 to 4 rings, rather than wedges.

Oranges in the Raw

Choose large juicy oranges and serve chilled as you would fresh grapefruit for breakfast, allowing half per person. If you want them to be special sprinkle over a little orange liqueur before serving.

Greengage Mousse

Take a 1 lb, 4-oz (567-g) can of greengages or plums, drain and remove the stones. Purée in a processor or blender until smooth, then add a 5-oz (150-g) carton of plain yogurt and ¼ pint (150 ml) whipping cream. Blend together, turn into a glass serving dish and chill. Serve with shortbread fingers (see page 188).

Serves 4

Knickerbocker Glory

Take a tall glass or wine glass per person (probably child) and then layer up vanilla and strawberry ice cream with canned fruit and a little jelly. Finally top with cream (use the aerosol canned variety for speed), sprinkle with nuts and serve with a couple of wafer biscuits.

Monte Bianco

Cut 2 small sponge cakes into small cubes about the size of a sugar lump and divide between 4 individual glasses and sprinkle each with a little sweet sherry. Put the contents of a 17-oz (500-g) can of sweetened chestnut purée in a bowl with 3 tablespoons double cream and beat well until blended. Divide this mixture between the glasses, shaping with a fork so that it forms a nest. Lightly whisk about ¼ pint (150 ml) double cream and pile into the centre of each nest and sprinkle with flaked almonds.

Serves 4

Ginger Biscuit Roll

Put ¼ pint (150 ml) double cream in a bowl and whisk until it forms stiff peaks and use to sandwich 8 oz (225 g) of ginger biscuits together to form a long roll. Place on a serving dish and leave in the refrigerator overnight. Next day whisk ¼ pint (150 ml) whipping cream until thick and use to cover the ginger biscuits. If liked decorate with small pieces of stem ginger. Cut into diagonal slices to serve.

Serves 4

Summer Layer Pudding

Melt 2 oz (50 g) butter in a small pan and stir in 6 oz (175 g) white breadcrumbs. Fry over a low heat until crisp and golden. Stir in 2 oz (50 g) demerara sugar and leave to cool. Place alternate layers of breadcrumbs with a 14-oz (397-g) can apple and blackcurrant pie filling in a dish, finishing with a layer of crumbs. Leave in a cool place to chill and then serve with cream.

Serves 4

Connaught Rice

Whisk ¼ pint (150 ml) double cream until it forms soft peaks. Whisk 1 egg white until stiff. Turn a 15-oz (425-g) can creamed rice into a bowl and fold in the cream and egg white and divide between 6 individual glasses. Drain a 15-oz (425-g) can of apricots and place the fruit on top of the rice. Take ¼ pint (150 ml) juice and blend a little of it with an egg yolk, a spoonful of sugar and 2 level teaspoons caster sugar. Bring the rest to the boil and then pour onto the egg mixture. Return to the pan, stirring until thick, then spoon over the apricots.

Serves 6

Fruity Ice Cream

Squeeze the juice from 1 orange and place in a small saucepan with 2 oz (50 g) of seedless raisins, 2 oz (50 g) glacé cherries and 2 oz (50 g) chopped walnuts. Bring to the boil slowly so that the fruit absorbs the orange juice and plumps up. Take a 17 fluid oz (500 ml) block vanilla ice cream, put in a bowl and soften and then stir in the fruit and mix thoroughly. Spoon into an ice cube tray and freeze until firm. Serve with wafers.

Serves 4

Peach Mallow

Drain a 15-oz (425-g) can white peach halves and place cut side up in an ovenproof serving dish. Put a little brandy in the centre of each peach half and then top each with 2 marshmallows. Put into the oven at about 425°F, 220°C, gas mark 7 for about 5 minutes or until the marshmallows are golden brown.

Serves 3 to 4

Baked Alaska

Put a 7-inch (17.5-cm) sponge flan case (see page 181) on an ovenproof plate and sprinkle with 2 tablespoons sherry. Arrange slices of your favourite ice cream on the flan. Whisk 2 egg whites until stiff and then whisk in 4 oz (100 g) caster sugar a teaspoonful at a time. Spread the meringue all over the ice cream so that it is completely sealed and then bake in a well preheated hot oven at 450°F, 230°C, gas mark 8 until the meringue is tinged a pale golden brown (about 3 minutes). Serve at once.

Serves 4 to 6

Cherry Mountain

Take 6 individual meringue baskets (see page 185) and place on individual dishes. Whisk ½ pint (300 ml) whipping cream until thick and forms soft peaks, spread over the base of the meringues and then top with a spoonful of cherry pie filling, piling it up in the centre.

Serves 6

Lychee, Lime and Kiwi Fruit Salad

Open a large can of lychees, and tip into a glass bowl. Peel and slice 2 kiwi fruits and add to the bowl. Squeeze in the juice from half a lime and then slice the remaining half lime very thinly (adding any juice to the bowl). Quarter, core and slice 2 green eating apples, stir into the fruit and then decorate the dish with the slices of lime. If time allows chill before serving.

Serves about 4

Black Cherry Slice

Split an 8-inch (20-cm) fatless sponge and place the base on a serving dish and sprinkle with a little sherry. Top with a can of cherry pie filling and whipped cream. Cover with the other piece of sponge and dust with icing sugar.

Serve cut in 8 wedges

Fresh Lemon Slice

Split an 8-inch (20-cm) fatless sponge and then sandwich together with ¼ pint (150 ml) whipped cream blended with 3 tablespoons lemon curd or bought lemon cheese. Dust with icing sugar.

Serves 8

Mint Chocolate Special

In our house mint chocolate chip ice cream – the bought kind – is always popular. In the summer to save washing up serve in cornets in scoopfuls and then let them have their puddings in the garden so that all the drips go on the grass and not on your carpet!

Fresh Fruit

The most simple pudding of all. Instead of offering the usual fruit bowl, serve just one variety of fruit in season, for example peaches when they are at their best and cheapest, or those wonderful tiny seedless grapes in the late summer when they are really sweet. Arrange on vine leaves so they look inviting. Ripe plums are delicious raw so don't always think you have to go to the bother of cooking them.

Fresh Pineapple in Kirsch (or Brandy or Cointreau)

Cut off the green top and base of the pineapple, slice off the peel and cut into slices, removing the core in the centre of each slice with an apple corer. Arrange in a glass dish, sprinkle with a little caster sugar and Kirsch and chill.

Serves 4 to 6

Fast Strawberry Fool

Make this when strawberries are very plentiful or rather too ripe to use for other things. Mash 8 oz (225 g) very ripe strawberries with a potato masher and sweeten with a little icing sugar. Stir into ½ pint (300 ml) soft vanilla ice cream, divide between 4 glass dishes and serve at once.

Serves 4

Just Fried Bananas

Fry small slightly under-ripe bananas in butter, allowing 2 per person, and then serve straight from the pan sprinkled with demerara sugar. Nice with cream.

Poire Hélène

Serve scoops of vanilla ice cream on either poached or canned pears in individual glasses and top with a hot chocolate sauce (see page 153). Serve at once.

Cherries Jubilee

Serve vanilla ice cream in scoops or slices in individual dishes or plates and spoon over some drained black cherries. Heat 4 tablespoons brandy in a pan, set alight and pour over the cherries just before serving.

Coupe Jacques

Place some fruit salad or cocktail in the base of individual serving dishes and put a scoop of strawberry or vanilla ice cream on top. Pipe a swirl of cream on each portion and serve with wafer biscuits.

BASICS FOR SPEED

The wise cook never finds her cupboard bare. The secret of fast cooking is in the freezer and the store cupboard. You gain enormous confidence from the knowledge that you can lay your hands on the ingredients you want at a moment's notice, and it is wise to devote some time and thought to keeping up your supply of basics, so that you will never be at a loss for the makings of a fast pudding.

The recipes that follow are all for the basics that you can make days, weeks or sometimes even months ahead, and store until you need them.

Pastry keeps well in the freezer, in blocks convenient for use. Bought pastry is very useful, but home-made gives more scope for variations – sweet, rich, extra short and so on – to suit different dishes. Make a big batch of pastry at a time and freeze some uncooked as flan cases or tartlet cases. You can of course buy these if you are short of time.

Also freeze sponge flan cases, sponge layers ready for filling, sponge biscuits and fingers, either bought or home-made.

Home-made meringues are infinitely better than the bought kind. I prefer them to be a very pale golden colour rather than the snow white ones that come from the shops. Make them in different sizes, from tiny ones to decorate a trifle or mousse, to large basket shapes to be filled with cream and sauces for topping it, fruit purées and cream.

In the larder canned fruit is always useful, as well as a good collection of biscuits, shortbread and almond fingers, made at home if you have time.

Do keep nuts in the freezer, whole ones and ground. They freeze well and you will be surprised how often you will use them.

178

Shortcrust Pastry Crumbs

Make up the pastry as crumbs and then store in a bag or plastic container in the refrigerator until required. It will keep for up to 4 weeks in the refrigerator, and for up to 6 months in the freezer. If using for pastry add about 6 tablespoons cold water and mix to a firm dough, or for a crumble add 2 oz (50 g) granulated or demerara sugar to each 8 oz (225 g) crumbs.

1 lb (450 g) plain flour
8 oz (225 g) soft margarine

Place the flour in a large bowl, add the soft margarine and rub in with the fingertips until the mixture resembles fine breadcrumbs. Either use or store in the refrigerator until required.

Makes 1½ lb (675 g) pastry crumbs

Basic Victoria Sandwich

Made by the all-in-one method, sponge cakes are perfect to have on hand, either in the store cupboard or freezer. Serve with coffee at the end of a meal instead of pudding or they can easily be made into a fruit gâteau for the unexpected visitor (see page 98).

Preparation time about 5 minutes
Cooking time about 25 to 30 minutes

4 oz (100 g) soft margarine
4 oz (100 g) caster sugar
2 large eggs, beaten
4 oz (100 g) self-raising flour
1 level teaspoon baking powder

Heat the oven to 350°F, 180°C, gas mark 4. Grease and line with greased greaseproof paper the bases of 2×7-inch (17.5-cm) straight sided sandwich tins.

Place all the ingredients in a large bowl and beat well for about 2 minutes, until blended and smooth. Divide between the tins and smooth the tops. Bake in the oven for 25 to 30 minutes. When the cake is cooked it will be a pale golden colour and the centre of the sponge will spring back into place when lightly pressed with the finger.

Turn out onto a wire rack to cool and then remove the paper. Store until required.

Chocolate Sandwich

First blend 1 rounded tablespoon cocoa with 2 tablespoons hot water in the bowl. Cool and then add the remaining ingredients and proceed as above.

Sponge Flan Case

I find it very convenient to keep a couple of these ready in the freezer. When short of time they can be used in place of a pastry case and thaw out very quickly in a warm room.

Making time about 15 minutes
Cooking time about 15 to 20 minutes

2 eggs
2 oz (50 g) caster sugar
2 oz (50 g) self-raising flour

Heat the oven to 375°F, 190°C, gas mark 5. Grease thoroughly and then dust well with flour a 7-inch (17.5-cm) sponge flan tin.

Put the eggs and sugar in a large heatproof bowl over a pan of hot water and whisk until the mixture is thick and creamy and leaves a thick trail when the whisk is lifted from the mixture. Remove from the heat and whisk for a further 2 minutes.

Sieve in the flour and very carefully fold it in with a metal spoon. Turn into the prepared tin and then bake in the oven for about 15 to 20 minutes when the mixture will be risen and a pale golden brown and the top will spring back when lightly pressed with a finger. Leave to cool in the tin for 2 to 3 minutes then turn out onto a wire rack and leave to cool.

Sponge Drops or Fingers

These use more or less the same basic ingredients but the method is different. Again they freeze well, and are handy to serve with fruit salads and whips.

Making time about 10 minutes
Cooking time about 12 to 15 minutes

2 eggs
2 oz (50 g) caster sugar
2 oz (50 g) self-raising flour
2 teaspoons lemon juice

Heat the oven to 350°F, 180°C, gas mark 4. Thoroughly grease and then flour 2 baking trays.

Separate the eggs and place the yolks in a bowl with the sugar and beat together with a wooden spoon until thick and creamy. Whisk the egg whites with a rotary or electric hand whisk until stiff. Fold the flour into the egg yolks with the lemon juice, then carefully fold through the egg whites using a metal spoon.

Place the mixture in a piping bag fitted with a ½ inch (1.25 cm) plain pipe and pipe the mixture onto the baking tray in 1½ inch (3.75 cm) drops, well spaced, or 8 on each tray. If you are in a hurry drop blobs using a dessertspoon instead of piping, but the shape won't be as even. If making sponge fingers pipe into fingers about 3 to 4 inches (7.5 to 10 cm) long, and you will get about 9 or 10 on each baking tray.

Bake in the oven for 12 to 15 minutes or until a pale golden brown. The sponge fingers will take less time then the drops. If liked sprinkle the drops or fingers with a little sieved icing sugar before baking. Lift off the baking tray and leave to cool on a wire rack until cold then store in an airtight tin or in the freezer.

Makes about 16 sponge drops or about 18 to 20 sponge fingers

Danish Cream

This is an alternative to custard and not as rich as cream. Serve very cold. A good way of using up left-over custard.

Preparation time about 2 to 3 minutes.

½ pint (300 ml) thick cold custard
¼ pint (150 ml) single cream

Place the custard in a processor or blender and run until smooth, add the cream and process again until blended.

Turn into a serving dish and place in the refrigerator until very cold before serving.

Makes ¾ pint (450 ml)

Meringues

Meringues are very versatile, and you can use this basic recipe to make any number of dishes. When cooked store in an airtight tin until required.

Preparation time about 10 minutes
Cooking time about 3 to 4 hours

> *3 egg whites*
> *6 oz (175 g) caster sugar*
> *whipped cream*

Heat the oven to 200°F, 100°C, gas mark ¼, and line 2 baking trays with silicone paper.

Place the egg whites in a large bowl and whisk on high speed with an electric or hand rotary whisk until they form soft peaks and then add the sugar a teaspoonful at a time. Continue whisking until all the sugar has been added. Using 2 dessertspoons, spoon the meringue out onto the trays putting 9 meringues on each tray.

Bake in the oven for 3 to 4 hours until the meringues are firm and dry and will easily lift from the paper. They will be a very pale off-white or slightly darker. Whisk the cream until thick and use to sandwich the meringues together.

Makes 9 double meringues

Brown Meringues

Make as above but use 6 oz (175 g) light soft brown sugar or the same quantity of sugar but half light soft brown sugar and half caster sugar, sieved together.

Meringue Layer

Make the basic meringue mixture and spread out onto the baking trays in 2×8-inch (20-cm) circles. Cook for about 1½ hours in the oven and then turn off the heat and allow to continue cooking in the cooling oven until quite cold. Sandwich together with a mixture of fruit and cream and decorate the top with swirls of cream and a few reserved pieces of fruit.

Tiny Meringues

Prepare the basic meringue mixture using 2 egg whites and 4 oz (100 g) caster sugar and then pipe the mixture with a large rose pipe onto 2 baking trays in rosettes about 1 inch (2.5 cm) in diameter. Bake for 1 hour and then turn off the heat and leave to cool in the oven.

Makes about 32 tiny meringues

Meringue Basket

Make up the basic meringue mixture and then place in a large piping bag fitted with a large rose pipe and fill an 8 inch (20 cm) circle with the meringue to make a flat base. Pipe rosettes of meringue around the edge to build up the sides. Bake in the oven for 3 to 4 hours. The basket may be filled with any fresh fruit and cream.

Serves 6 to 8

Individual Meringue Baskets

Use the same method as above but make 6 individual meringue baskets using a 4 inch (10 cm) base. If time is short put the meringue on the baking tray in 6 heaps and hollow out the centres to make rough baskets. Bake in the oven for 3 to 4 hours. Serve filled with fruit and cream.

Pancakes

The boys make twice this recipe at least and keep it in a jug in the refrigerator, then they make their own pancakes for puddings in the holidays. We like them best with lemon and sugar. One of the easiest fast puddings – if there is any left it can also be used for Yorkshire pudding, and you can serve it sweet with syrup instead of gravy.

To freeze, pack them in convenient numbers (4 to 8 are enough for a meal). Wrap each batch in foil. If you are likely to want to use them without thawing them first put a piece of greaseproof paper or foil between each pancake, then with care you can prise them apart while they are still frozen.

Preparation time about 5 minutes
Cooking time about 2 minutes for each pancake

caster sugar
4 oz (100 g) plain flour
1 egg, beaten
½ pint (300 ml) milk and water mixed
1 tablespoon salad oil
oil for frying
lemon juice

Sprinkle the caster sugar on a sheet of greaseproof paper and put on one side. Put flour in a bowl and make a well in the centre. Add the egg and gradually stir in half the milk and water mixture. Using a whisk blend in the flour from the sides of the bowl. Beat well until the mixture is smooth. Stir in the remaining liquid and oil.

Heat a little oil in a 7-inch (17.5-cm) frying pan. When hot pour off any excess oil and spoon about 2 tablespoons of the batter into the pan. Tip and rotate the pan so that the batter spreads out and thinly covers the bottom of the pan. Cook the pancakes for a minute, until pale brown underneath, then turn over with a palette knife and cook for a minute. Invert the pancake onto sugared paper, sprinkle with lemon juice and roll up. Place on a hot serving dish and keep warm whilst making more in the same way.

Makes 8 to 10 pancakes

Almond Biscuits

I like to keep these in an airtight tin ready to serve with ice cream dishes, mousses, syllabub and zabaglione.

Preparation time about 10 minutes
Cooking time about 8 minutes

3 oz (75 g) butter
3 oz (75 g) caster sugar
2 oz (50 g) plain flour
3 oz (75 g) almonds, finely shredded

Heat the oven to 400°F, 200°C, gas mark 6. Well butter 4 baking trays.

Cream the butter and sugar together until light and fluffy, then work in the flour with the almonds. Put the mixture in teaspoonfuls, 6 to a tray and well spaced, and then flatten with a wet fork.

Bake in the oven for about 8 minutes so that the biscuits are just a pale colour around the edge. Remove from the oven and leave for a few minutes to cool and then lift onto a wire cooling rack.

Store in a tin until required.

Makes 24 biscuits

Shortbread Fingers

Very useful to keep on hand. They store well in an airtight tin and are very useful to serve with whips, mousses or fools. (*See picture facing page 65.*)

Making time about 10 minutes
Cooking time about 15 to 20 minutes

4 oz (100 g) plain flour
2 oz (50 g) ground rice
4 oz (100 g) butter
2 oz (50 g) caster sugar

Heat the oven to 325°F, 160°C, gas mark 3. Lightly grease an 11×7 inch (27.5×17.5 cm) shallow tin.

Sieve the flour and ground rice together. Cream the butter with the caster sugar until light and fluffy and then work in the flour and ground rice. Knead well together, then press into the tin evenly, using the back of a damp spoon or your knuckles.

Bake in the oven for about 15 to 20 minutes or until the shortbread is a very pale golden brown. Remove from the oven and cut into 16 fingers, leave to cool in the tin and then remove and store in an airtight tin.

Makes 16 shortbread fingers

Small Macaroons

These are so handy to have in the cupboard and are ideal to put in a trifle instead of sponge cakes.

Preparation time about 10 minutes
Cooking time about 12 to 15 minutes

2 large egg whites
3 oz (75 g) caster sugar
3 oz (75 g) ground almonds
1 oz (25 g) cornflour

Heat the oven to 375°F, 190°C, gas mark 5. Line 2 baking trays with silicone paper.

Whisk the egg whites until stiff and then whisk in half the sugar a teaspoonful at a time. Sieve the remaining sugar with the ground almonds and cornflour so that they are evenly mixed and then fold into the meringue with a metal spoon.

Place the mixture in teaspoonfuls on the baking trays, putting about 10 heaps on each tray, and smooth flat with the back of the teaspoon. Bake in the oven for about 12 to 15 minutes until a pale golden brown. Leave to cool on a wire rack.

These may be stored in the deep freeze in a plastic container, covered and labelled.

Makes about 20 small macaroons

Index

191